The
WEEKEND
GARDENER

Reader's Digest

The WEEKEND GARDENER

 Reader's Digest

THE READER'S DIGEST ASSOCIATION, INC.
Pleasantville, New York/Montreal

A READER'S DIGEST BOOK

Conceived, edited, and designed by
Collins & Brown Limited

Copyright © 1998 Collins & Brown Limited
Text copyright © 1998 Susanna Longley

Editorial Director: Sarah Hoggett
Assistant Editor: Corinne Asghar
Art Director: Roger Bristow
Designed by: Steve Wooster
Senior Art Editor: Julia Ward-Hastelow
Designers: Alison Lee, Ian Merrill
DTP Designer: Ed Lawrance
Photography: Sampson Lloyd
Additional Photography: Geoff Dann, Mark Gatehouse
Illustrators: Vanessa Luff, Martine Collings
Diagrams: David Ashby
Picture Adminstration: Tiffany Jenkins

Library of Congress Cataloging in Publication Data

Longley, Susanna.
The weekend gardener : simple weekend projects for a great garden
/ Susanna Longley.
    p. cm.
Includes index.
ISBN 0-7621-0018-4
1. Landscape gardening. 2. Gardening. I. Title.
SB473. L655 1998
635.9 – dc21   97-38729

Printed in Italy

Contents

Planning Your Weekend Garden

WHETHER WE LIKE it or not, most of us are "weekend gardeners," fitting all of our gardening efforts into a few precious hours along with other domestic chores, such as shopping and housework, — and, of course, relaxing with family and friends. But having only a limited amount of time shouldn't entail any lowering of quality. It simply means that you have to tailor the garden to suit your own resources and requirements.

The Weekend Gardener is designed to help you do just that. A lot of practical gardening books are over-ambitious: they seem to assume that everyone wants to go back to the drawing board, ripping out established plants and temporarily installing a cement mixer in their place while the entire site is relandscaped. *The Weekend Gardener*, on the other hand, recognizes that few people have the time, energy, or resources for this. Instead, it encourages you to look for ways of enhancing what you already have through a series of small, manageable projects that you can carry out at a time that suits your schedule.

Start by asking yourself a series of questions in order to work out exactly what you want from your garden:

How much time can I spend gardening?

If you're limited to just a few hours each week, then you need low-maintenance designs, easy-care plants that suit the situation in which you plant them, and projects for which the basic groundwork can be done in a matter of hours rather than days. All the projects in this book fall into those categories, leaving you time to relax and enjoy the fruits of your labors.

Garden for pleasure!
Gardening should be fun! Whether you enjoy pottering around for hours (above) or prefer quick-and-easy, instant results, such as planting a container (right), use the projects in The Weekend Gardener *to help you plan your garden so that you get the maximum enjoyment out of it.*

Quick and easy
Tailor your gardening projects to fit the time you have available. Containers are a quick way of bringing instantly mature plantings to your garden.

What aspects of gardening do I enjoy?

Do you like pottering around, getting your hands dirty and putting in different plants for each season — or would you prefer to establish a core of permanent plants that, once planted, need very little upkeep? Do you find mowing the lawn a good way of relaxing after a hard week's work — or does the thought of having to spend your precious Sunday mornings cutting the grass discourage you? Make a list of the activities you do and don't enjoy, and use it as the basis for revamping certain areas of your garden, if necessary, so that you can get the maximum enjoyment out of your gardening. Before you embark on any of the projects in this book, check the Project Planner and Maintenance boxes (see pages 10–11) to see what you're getting yourself into — and if you don't like the sound of it, don't do it!

How do I plan to use my garden?

Is it primarily a place to relax? If so, attractive, planting schemes that are easy to care for may be your top priority. Or is it somewhere for the kids to play? In that case, a large grassy area, surrounded by robust shrubs

Design a garden that suits your needs
Rather than being a slave to other people's ideas of what a garden should be, make sure that your garden fits in with your tastes and lifestyle. Whether you want it to be a horticultural showpiece with luxuriant herbaceous borders (above) or a place to relax and enjoy the sunshine (left) is entirely your decision.

and ground-cover plants that can withstand trampling from young feet, might be the best answer. Again, make a list of your personal priorities, rather than copying designs that do not fit in with your family's needs.

Be prepared to adapt your garden to suit your changing circumstances. Once the kids have grown up and left home, you can plant over the play area or pave it to create a stylish-looking patio. If you retire from full-time work, you will probably have more leisure time – and the carefully nurtured herbaceous border that you've always dreamed of is suddenly within your grasp. The projects in *The Weekend Gardener* give you plenty of scope for quick-and-easy make-overs that will transform your garden in a short space of time.

What constraints does my garden impose?

By choosing plants that naturally thrive in your garden's conditions – shade-tolerant species for a shaded site, for example – you are making life a lot easier for yourself as a weekend gardener, since happy plants require less maintenance. The Gardening Basics section (pages 12–51) shows you how to analyse the soil and other conditions that prevail in your garden. Each project makes it clear what conditions it is designed for. If you decide you would like to use plants other than the ones suggested, the plant lists on pages 182–185 are a useful starting point. Supplement this information by consulting a good plant reference manual before you

buy anything, also check the label that accompanies potted plants.

Armed with a checklist of your own gardening priorities and conditions, you are now in a far better position to assess which of the projects in *The Weekend Gardener* meet your needs.

Design plantings that suit your garden
The Gardening Basics section (pages 12–51) explains how to analyse the conditions that prevail in your garden, so you can choose plants and designs that will be successful.

About This Book

THE WEEKEND GARDENER begins with a short introduction to basic gardening skills, which covers techniques for improving your soil, sowing seed, planting everything from bulbs to trees, watering, and general maintenance such as staking and pruning. Use this section as a handy reference source whenever you're unsure about how to do something. The step-by-step projects in the book refer you to the Gardening Basics section for information on routine gardening tasks.

This section ends with The Weekend Gardener's Calendar, which tells you what routine gardening tasks you should be doing throughout the year. When you're short of time, planning ahead to maximize what little time you have is essential. Get into the habit of checking this calendar every month, using it as a reminder of what you need to do. Carrying out the right task at the right time will save you time in the long run: prune a shrub at the right time of year and you'll keep it looking neat and tidy and encourage bushy growth, but

Gardening basics section
The Gardening Basics section (pages 12–51) sets out in an easy-to-follow format all the essential practical information that you are likely to need as a weekend gardener.

Step-by-step photographs
Step-by-step photographs and instructions make routine gardening tasks easy for everyone to follow.

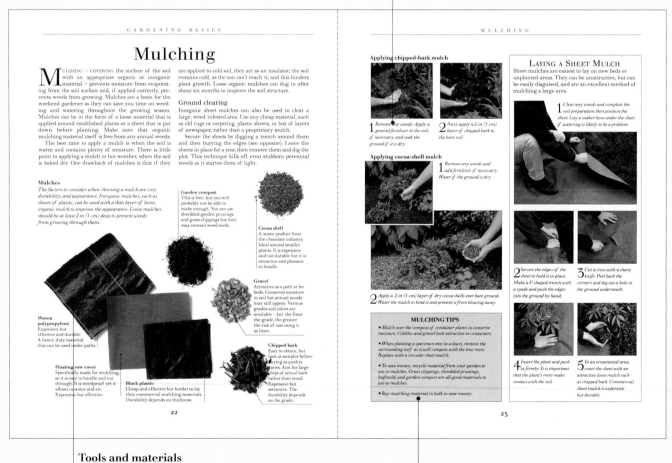

Tools and materials
Color photographs of gardening tools and materials are included throughout, so that you can devise your own weekend gardener's tool kit.

Tips
Useful tips are displayed in special feature boxes for easy reference.

leave it for a year or two and you'll find that you have a much larger task on your hands. By planning your garden maintenance in advance, you can spread tasks over several weekends rather than trying to blitz everything in a single day at the end of the growing season in preparation for winter.

The core of *The Weekend Gardener* is a series of project-based chapters with a unique cross-referencing system to help you decide which projects are most appropriate to your own garden. All the projects are designed to be achievable within one weekend at the most; many take only an hour or two.

Each of the first five projects chapters begins with a series of questions setting out common gardening problems. Some of these problems relate to aesthetic or design points (for example, "Is your lawn a harsh, geometric shape?"), while others touch on horticultural considerations (for example, "Do you have a mature tree under which nothing grows well?"). You are then referred to a specific project or projects that will help you to answer the question. Use these pages for both practical help and as inspiration; they are intended to open your eyes to possibilities that you might never have considered.

Question-and-answer pages
These question-and-answer pages are a unique feature of The Weekend Gardener. *By setting out typical problems that many people encounter in their gardens, they are designed to help you choose projects that are appropriate to your own situation.*

Typical gardening problem
Questions set out typical gardening problems or situations that you might encounter in your own garden.

Ideas for Improving Walls, Fences, and Hedges

THE EXTERNAL boundaries of your garden – the walls, fences, and hedges – provide the basic framework against which all of your plantings are seen. They also have a practical effect on the microclimate of your garden, creating shelter and shade and therefore influencing the type of plants that you can grow. When you choose plants, you need to think not only about factors such as shade, but also about aesthetic considerations – how your plants will blend in or contrast with the boundaries in terms of their color and texture.

Something that many people overlook is that walls, fences, and hedges can also be used as internal divisions – separating a patio area from the rest of the garden, or creating a secluded corner where you can enjoy the afternoon sunshine.

The questions on these two pages are designed to help you pinpoint ways in which you can improve existing boundaries, or create new ones, in order to enhance your garden. Each one is backed up by a step-by-step project that includes suggestions for plants that you might like to use in your own garden.

? Does your garden feel too open?
Set up boundaries within the garden to create a separate "garden room" or a series of "rooms" and make it more interesting to walk through. *Right:* This garden sanctuary is created by 7-ft (2.1 m) high yew hedging. The petunias and potted marguerite daisies match the striking white statue. SEE *A Garden Divider, page 110; Formal Hedge, page 114.*

? Does your front-yard fence look dilapidated?
With a minimum of practical skills, you can create an informal fence that also makes the perfect frame for plants to grow on and around. SEE *Front-Yard Boundary, page 118.*

? Do buildings enclose or overlook your garden?
Raise the height of boundary walls and fences (be sure to check any local ordinances) and grow climbers up them to make them look more attractive. *Above:* A trellis, covered in the beautiful *Rosa* 'Handel', increases the height of the low wall and prevents the garden from being overlooked. SEE *Heightening a Wall with Trellis, page 104*

? Is your hedge an expanse of single color?
Plant a flowering hedge or train a succession of flowering climbers through an evergreen hedge to give seasonal variety and color. *Above:* The colorful splendor of this beautiful garden overflows into the hedges. The clipped, dark-green yew cone is enhanced by the flame-colored nasturtium. SEE *Adding Color to Green Hedges, page 108; Informal Boundary Hedge, page 112.*

? Do your bed and border edges look untidy?
Plant a miniature hedge to define the edges. *Left:* This miniature box hedge makes a neat edging to the bed and hides the bare rose stems. Alpine daisies and catmint cascade over the wall in front of the hedge. SEE *Defining Your Beds, page 116.*

? Do you have a fence or boundary that is bare and boring?
Use trellis panels to break up a blank wall area and train climbers and wall shrubs through the trellis to soften the edges. If the wall gets the sun, you can create a scented sitting area. SEE *Enhancing a Bare Wall, page 102; Plants for a Sunny Wall, page 106.*

100

101

Quick-and-easy answers
The solution to each question is a quick-and-easy project that you can carry out over the course of a single weekend.

Cross-references
By following up the cross-references, you can turn to a project or projects within the chapter for help in solving your gardening problem. Sometimes there are several options open to you.

ABOUT THIS BOOK (continued)

Each project features an illustration that shows you what it will look like once the plants have reached maturity. Read the introduction to the project to find out what sort of situation it is suitable for and what benefits it will bring to your garden. Many of the projects contain Alternative Plantings so that you can adapt the design to a different situation or a different color scheme. Not everyone has the same requirements, but *The Weekend Gardener* gives you the flexibility to adapt designs to suit your own situation.

Once you have decided which projects you would like to do, read through the project to be sure you know what's involved before you start. This is important: not only do you need to know how to carry out the project, but you should also be aware of what you will need to do to maintain it. Draw up a shopping list of tools, materials, and plants – and you're ready to begin!

The final chapter gives ideas for building a garden around a specific theme. The four shown here are the most popular types of themed garden – herb gardens,

Projects for the weekend gardener
The Weekend Gardener *contains around 50 projects to improve your garden that can be completed within a single weekend; many take only an hour or two. All are clearly set out with full step-by-step instructions.*

Plant lists
The plant lists (pages 182–185) should be your first port of call if you want to check whether or not a particular plant will work in the situation for which you have chosen it.

PLANTS FOR DIFFERENT PURPOSES

Plants for Different Purposes

listed (for example, the bay ... but only this

The benefits of each project
The introductory text sets out the benefits each project will bring to your garden and, where appropriate, includes useful practical information on such topics as plant choices and garden design.

where
attract
free (a
If
genus
genu
incl
able
gen
lab
wh
to

BEDS AND BORDERS

Creating a Focal Point
SCENTED LILY AND ROSE ARBOR

A FREE-STANDING ARBOR or arch swathed in flowers brings several benefits to a garden: it can be used to divide the garden into separate areas, to frame a striking view, or to distract attention from an unattractive one. Beyond these, it provides a focal point – a dramatic, eye-catching feature that makes a strong design statement.

You can make your own arch, but it is far easier to buy one in kit form from a garden center. There is a wide range to choose from – in wood and metal – and to suit all budgets. Once you have made sure that the arch is well anchored in the ground, you can start to train climbing plants to grow up and around it.

An arch is a particularly effective way of displaying such scented climbers as roses or honeysuckle, since you benefit from wafts of perfume every time you pass through it. Some rose varieties, particularly if they are trained over a wall or solid surface, are prone to mildew in humid conditions. However, growing them over an arch can help prevent this problem, since air is able to circulate freely through the plants' stems.

Fragrant pink and white arch
This arch is smothered in fragrant pink roses, while pots of lilies clothe the base. Geraniums and sweet violets cover the ground and help to minimize weed growth.

Specially commissioned illustrations
A full-color illustration depicts each planting scheme once it has reached maturity.

Plant photographs
Color photographs show the suggested plants in close-up detail for ease of identification.

1 Pink rambler rose such as *Rosa* 'New Dawn'

2 Madonna lily (*Lilium candidum*)

3 Pink climbing rose such as *Rosa* 'Zéphirine Drouhin'

4 *Geranium* x *magnificum*

5 Sweet violet (*Viola odorata*), shown here in flower in spring

130

wildflower gardens, woodland gardens, and water gardens – though there are, of course, many other types of garden that you could treat in this way and this section should inspire you to come up with your own ideas.

Finally, you will find plant lists that tell you which plants grow best in particular situations. If you want to substitute other plants for the ones suggested in *The Weekend Gardener*, or if you want to devise your own planting schemes, your first step should be to refer to these lists. They will save you a lot of time plowing

through more detailed plant reference books – although, of course, you may want to use such books to supplement the information given here.

If you carry away just one message from this book, it should be that gardening is fun – and to achieve this, you need to make sure that your garden works for you, not the other way round. Decide on your own personal priorities and adapt your garden, if necessary, to allow you to make the most of your precious free time. Above all, enjoy being a Weekend Gardener!

Maintenance
Maintenance tips tell you how to keep each project looking its best.

Time scale
The Time Scale tells you roughly how long each project takes, so that you can plan your weekend accordingly.

Tools and materials
The Tools and Materials list sets out all the equipment you need for each project, so that you can make sure you have everything you need before you start.

Clear, step-by-step instructions
Easy-to-follow instructions take you through the different stages of each project step by step.

Alternative Plantings
Many of the projects feature Alternative Plantings, allowing you to vary the suggested planting scheme to suit your own tastes and requirements – changing the color, perhaps, or adapting the plants from sun-loving species to shade-tolerant ones.

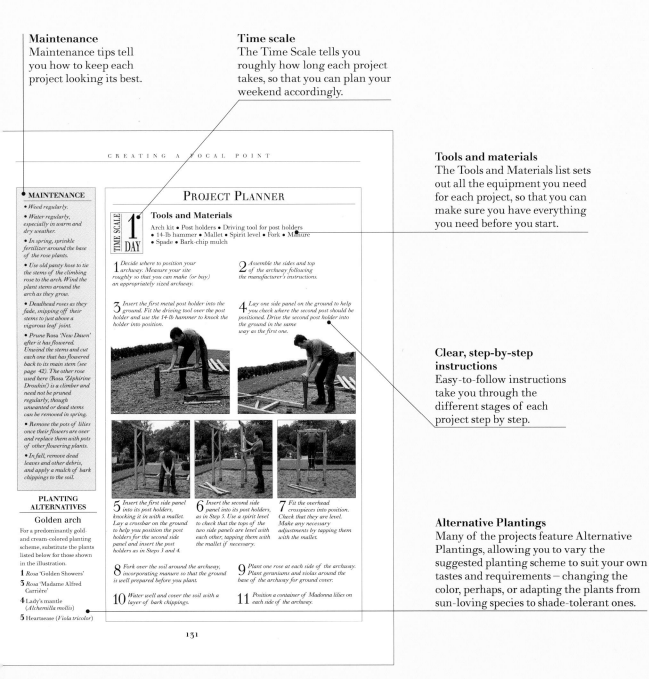

CREATING A FOCAL POINT

● MAINTENANCE

• *Weed regularly.*

• *Water regularly, especially in warm and dry weather.*

• *In spring, sprinkle fertilizer around the base of the rose plants.*

• *Use old panty hose to tie the stems of the climbing rose to the arch. Wind the plant stems around the arch as they grow.*

• *Deadhead roses as they fade, snipping off their stems to just above a vigorous leaf joint.*

• *Prune Rosa 'New Dawn' after it has flowered. Unwind the stems and cut each one that has flowered back to its main stem (see page 42). The other rose used here (Rosa 'Zéphirine Drouhin') is a climber and need not be pruned regularly, though unwanted or dead stems can be removed in spring.*

• *Remove the pots of lilies once their flowers are over and replace them with pots of other flowering plants.*

• *In fall, remove dead leaves and other debris, and apply a mulch of bark chippings to the soil.*

PLANTING ALTERNATIVES

Golden arch

For a predominantly gold- and cream-colored planting scheme, substitute the plants listed below for those shown in the illustration.

1 *Rosa 'Golden Showers'*

3 *Rosa 'Madame Alfred Carrière'*

4 *Lady's mantle (Alchemilla mollis)*

5 Heartsease (*Viola tricolor*)

PROJECT PLANNER

TIME SCALE **1 DAY**

Tools and Materials

Arch kit • Post holders • Driving tool for post holders • 14-lb hammer • Mallet • Spirit level • Fork • Manure • Spade • Bark-chip mulch

1 *Decide where to position your archway. Measure your site roughly so that you can make (or buy) an appropriately sized archway.*

2 *Assemble the sides and top of the archway following the manufacturer's instructions.*

3 *Insert the first metal post holder into the ground. Fit the driving tool over the post holder and use the 14-lb hammer to knock the holder into position.*

4 *Lay one side panel on the ground to help you check where the second post should be positioned. Drive the second post holder into the ground in the same way as the first one.*

5 *Insert the first side panel into its post holders, knocking it in with a mallet. Lay a crossbar on the ground to help you position the post holders for the second side panel and insert the post holders as in Steps 3 and 4.*

6 *Insert the second side panel into its post holders, as in Step 5. Use a spirit level to check that the tops of the two side panels are level with each other, tapping them with the mallet if necessary.*

7 *Fit the overhead crosspieces into position. Check that they are level. Make any necessary adjustments by tapping them with the mallet.*

8 *Fork over the soil around the archway, incorporating manure so that the ground is well prepared before you plant.*

9 *Plant one rose at each side of the archway. Plant geraniums and violas around the base of the archway for ground cover.*

10 *Water well and cover the soil with a layer of bark chippings.*

11 *Position a container of Madonna lilies on each side of the archway.*

131

11

GARDENING BASICS

Basic but beautiful
*Using a few basic gardening techniques and some
careful planning, you can create a garden to be
proud of. These striking textures not only look
spectacular, but are easy to achieve.*

Getting to Know Your Garden

UNDERSTANDING THE conditions that exist in your garden – whether it is sunny or shaded, sheltered or exposed – and identifying the type of soil you have is the key to successful gardening. Plants that like your garden environment are more likely to thrive and less likely to succumb to pests and diseases.

How sunny or shaded is your garden?

Most gardens have both sunny and shaded areas. First, determine which parts of the garden catch the sun and which are in shade: the amount of sun or shade that your garden receives can change throughout the day and with the seasons. Next, make a note of the spots where your garden offers shelter from wind or where it is completely exposed. Observe and keep a log about the different parts of your garden throughout the year.

With this information, you can position your plants in the most appropriate situation.

What type of soil do you have?

Plant roots need a balanced supply of moisture, air, and nutrients, but the amount of each that is available to them depends on the soil type. There are a number of different types of soil and there may even be variations within your garden. The most common types are shown below to help you identify them.

The ability of a soil to hold air and water depends on the origin and size of its particles. Most garden soils contain particles derived from rocks or other minerals. Simply rubbing the soil between your fingertips will give you some idea of the size of the particles. Large particles, such as those found in sandy soils, feel gritty.

Soil types
Gardens, even in the same locality, can have very different soils. There may even be differences within your garden. Here are the most common soil types.

Peaty soil
Peaty soil is usually dark, wet, and acidic. It can produce excellent plant growth, but often lies wet in winter and dries out quickly in summer.

Clay soil
Clay soil is fertile and retains water. The particles are small with few air spaces. If worked when wet, clay soil can become compacted, which makes it harder for plants to grow. When hot, the surface of the clay can bake hard.

Loamy soil
This is the ideal soil for plant growth. The soil contains clay, so it is fertile, and sand, so it has good drainage.

Sandy soil
Sandy soil has large particles with lots of air spaces between them, making the soil light and easy to work. Water drains quickly through the soil, carrying with it water-soluble nutrients. The soil is dry and the fertility level is low.

Alkaline soil
Alkaline soil can be sandy or clay. Its chemical content (it is comprised of limestone) makes it harder for some plants to extract nutrients from it.

If the particles are very small, the soil feels smooth. A soil that can be molded into a ball is either loam or clay (see below). A few soils, such as peaty soil, have so much organic matter present that the size of any mineral particles is not relevant.

You can learn about your garden soil by handling it. Sandy soils will not stick together in a ball shape, while soils containing clay can be rolled into a ball (see below).

Making a soil ball

1 Knead the moist soil in your hands and work it into a ball. If it has a texture like putty and forms a ball, the soil contains clay.

2 Roll the ball into a sasuage shape and bend it around to form a ring. If this can be done, there is a high clay content (over 35 per cent) in the soil.

How well drained is your soil?

In addition to assessing your soil's particle size, you must also establish if there is a water source near by. In winter, dig a hole up to 2 ft (60 cm) deep. Fill the hole with water and cover it if rain is forecast. Note how long it takes for the water to drain. If the water drains away within 24 hours there is no drainage problem. If the soil is poorly drained, the hole will still contain water after 24 hours. In a free-draining soil, water drains in less than an hour. If more water seeps into the hole, there must be another source of water near by.

Plants vary greatly in their tolerance to waterlogging and to dryness at the roots. If your soil is very wet or very dry it will greatly affect the types of plants that will establish unless you take steps to improve it.

How acid or alkaline is your soil?

The acidity or alkalinity of your soil also affects the sort of plants that you can grow in your garden. Most plants prefer a soil that is slightly acid (pH 6.5), but there are exceptions, including rhododendrons, camellias, and some heathers. Other plants are able to tolerate more alkaline soils; these are sometimes known as "lime loving." Well-known lime-loving plants include aquilegias, clematis, marjoram, and veronicas. Most soils are between pH 5.5 and 7.5. In practice, you may not need to know the pH value as many test kits simply require you to match the color of a liquid with a description, such as "slightly acid."

TAKING A SOIL SAMPLE

You can get a rough idea of whether your soil is acid, alkaline, or neutral by using either a simple test kit or a soil meter. Test each bed or area separately, and take several readings at different points in each bed, averaging them out to obtain an overall reading. Conduct the test before adding manure or fertilizers and always use clean tools. A soil meter has a probe that allows you to take readings directly from the soil. Test kits can be cheaper and more reliable than basic soil meters.

1 Lay bamboo stakes on the surface of the soil in the shape of a W. Take a walnut-sized sample of soil at each end of each stake. You should have five samples to mix together.

2 Discard any stones or weeds and put the soil in a clean dish. Break up any lumps with your fingers and mix the sample up well.

3 Half fill the test tube with soil. Add water to fill and shake well. Allow the soil to settle, then take the soil reading.

4 Match the color of the solution to the color chart that is provided with the kit. The description or number next to the closest color match tells you the pH value of your soil.

Improving Your Soil

Your soil's characteristics may limit the plants you can choose for your garden. However, there are lots of things you can do to to improve your soil. Good-quality soil is a major asset, and it is worth preparing your soil before you begin planting. Soil that contains the correct balance of water, air, and nutrients will reduce the amount of maintenance you need to do and improve the performance of your plants.

Concentrate on improving the topsoil – from the surface down to one spade's depth – as few plant roots penetrate much deeper. Digging uncultivated ground will open up the soil, making it easier for plant roots to establish. If your topsoil is shallow, add soil improvers (see pages 17–19) each year. When planting trees and shrubs in shallow topsoil, dig a deep planting pit and fill with topsoil (from another part of the garden or bought in bags) so that they can root deeply.

If the soil is very poor quality, clear the topsoil and replace it with new soil before purchasing your plants.

You should see the benefits of improving your soil within a couple of years. Although annual applications of rotted organic matter will still be needed, the plants themselves will contribute to the soil. Plant roots can prevent light soils from getting washed away. Dead plant material can be collected and turned into compost, then returned to improve the soil.

Digging and raking tools
Tools for working the soil need to be durable, easy to clean, and comfortable to use. It is worth paying extra for good-quality tools.

Hand fork
Use for weeding and cultivating the soil around established plants.

Trowel
Use for planting small plants, such as perennials.

Garden fork
Use for breaking up and preparing soil. It can also be used to improve lawns (see page 77), move garden debris, and turn compost heaps. Smaller border forks are also available.

Spade
Use for preparing soil and digging planting holes for trees and shrubs. Border spades have a narrow base and are easier to use in established beds; they are also lighter.

Soil rake
Use for leveling outdoor seedbeds and breaking down clods of earth to a crumbly texture.

16

Soil profile

Soil consists of horizontal layers of different materials. Most plants occupy only the topsoil, so soil improvers, fertilizers, or lime, should be applied to this layer.

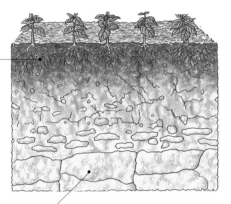

Topsoil
This is the fertile layer in which plants root. It contains organic matter and micro-organisms, critical for growing healthy plants. The topsoil should be at least one spade's depth.

Subsoil
This is often lighter in color and coarser in texture than topsoil. Avoid mixing subsoil into topsoil as it lacks organic matter and micro-organisms.

Soil improvers

There are many sources of organic matter that can be used to improve the soil structure. Garden waste can be recycled as compost or leafmold. You can use any leaves except conifer clippings, to make leafmold. Pack the leaves into a large black plastic bag, and moisten if necessary, punch a few holes in the plastic bag, and store for two years. Leaves rot slowly, so should be treated separately from other garden waste.

You may need to supplement garden compost or leafmold, as it can be difficult to make large quantities.

Alternative sources of organic waste include local stables or mushroom farms. You can also buy specially prepared bagged products from garden centers.

Prices vary greatly, so shop around if you have large areas of soil to treat. Consider the convenience of each product: some of the cheaper sources need to be prepared months in advance or are only available at certain times of year or in bulk quantities.

Apply soil improvers generously. Spread a 2-in (5-cm) layer over the bed, then dig in. Some materials also add nutrients, but the amounts vary and are not usually declared on the packaging.

Commercial soil improvers that you buy from garden centers or mail order companies can also be used, although you may not want to for ecological reasons. These are usually a blend of waste products, such as poultry manure and bark or peat. The products are often alkaline, so check the packaging for advice if you want to use them around acid-loving plants.

What soil needs

Topsoil should contain mineral particles, such as clay and sand, and lots of humus. Humus is formed when micro-organisms break down plant and animal material. It coats the soil and makes it easier to cultivate.

By digging in rotted organic matter you add air to the soil and produce humus. The soil will then hold moisture without becoming waterlogged. You should do this regardless of your soil type. As the humus decomposes, add bulky organic matter each year. If your soil is very acid or alkaline, you can help to redress the balance by adding particular soil improvers.

Improving alkaline soils

It is not easy to make alkaline soil more acidic. Adding peat helps to reduce acidity, while some nitrogen fertilizers, such as sulphate of ammonia, can make soils more acidic. Choose plants that thrive on limestone and grow acid-loving plants in containers of peat-based soil.

Improving acid soils

A slightly acidic soil (pH 6.5) is ideal for lawns, fruit, and many other plants. Very acidic soils (pH 5) can still grow certain plants, for example rhododendrons, camellias, heathers, and blueberries, but by adding lime (calcium carbonate) to reduce the acidity, you can grow a greater range of plants. This can be done at any time, except when manure is added or just before or after planting. Spent mushroom compost (see page 19) is also a good source of lime and organic matter.

Adding lime
Apply 4–8 oz (100–200 g) of lime (calcium carbonate) per sq yd (sq m). A convenient time to do this is when digging the ground in the fall. Dig or rake the lime into the soil. Test the soil the following spring to see if it is less acidic.

Improving peaty soils

A peaty soil, which is already acidic, does not need extra organic matter. However, you will need to add lime if you want to grow vegetables, as they prefer neutral or slightly alkaline soils. Peaty soils can be hard to rewet, so irrigate before they dry. Placing a couple of drops of liquid detergent in the water helps the soil to absorb moisture. Add extra fertilizer in the spring.

MAKING GARDEN COMPOST

Making compost is an excellent way of recycling household and garden waste. Buy or make a bin. The minimum size to generate enough heat is around 3 ft (1 m) square. Add material in 1-ft (30-cm) layers and water if dry. Add an activator between each layer to speed up the breakdown of the material. Activators include sulphate of ammonia, calcified seaweed, nettles, and comfrey leaves. Finish with a layer of garden soil. Store-bought bins come with a cover, but if you make your own bin it will need a cover, as heavy rain could turn the compost into a slimy mess.

1 Use a variety of materials to make compost, adding each in 6-in (15-cm) layers. Turn the material over with a digging fork every couple of months to speed up the decomposition process.

2 Cover the top layer of material with a waterproof sheet.

3 After three to six months the compost will be ready. Either dig it into the soil as a soil improver or apply on the surface as a mulch.

DO NOT COMPOST

The following should be excluded:

• *Food with grease or fat. Meat or fish waste.*

• *Coal ash from fires (wood ash can be used in small quantities).*

• *Diseased plant material, particularly if infected with viruses.*

• *Annual weeds in flower or with seedheads. Perennial weeds in flower or seed or their roots.*

Home and Garden Compost

Home-made compost is the most economic type of soil improver. Many materials from the garden and home can be recycled into garden compost. Here are the most useful:

Fruit and vegetable waste
Cooked or raw, tea leaves, coffee grinds, egg shells.

Pet litter
You can use hamster and rabbit litter but not cat and dog.

Newspaper or cardboard
Shred and wet to help them break down.

Green prunings
From bedding plants, deadheading, cutting down herbaceous plants. Woody prunings should be shredded first.

Hay, dry grass
Grass clippings are suitable if dried first or mixed with other material.

Dead leaves
Can be added in small quantities.

Nettles
Are useful for activating the compost.

Other Organic Soil Improvers

These are available in larger quantities than garden compost, and are invaluable for conditioning the soil.

Farmyard manure

A valuable soil improver but do not use fresh or it can scorch new roots. Fresh manure should be piled up (away from open water and children) for six months to a year before use. Horse or cow manure is the best for gardens; chicken manure can be very strong and give off ammonia.

Bark

Composted or chipped bark is a waste product from wood mills. It can be used to open up soil structure. Shredded prunings have similar properties. All are best composted before use.

Spent mushroom compost

This is used by commercial growers use for raising mushrooms. It is a mixture of horse manure, peat, and lime. It is a good soil improver for vegetable growing and helps to reduce acidity in the soil.

Improving Drainage

To open up air spaces in all types of soil, dig in rotted organic matter. For heavy clay soil, dig in horticultural sand. It is expensive and incorporating it can be hard work but, unlike adding organic matter, it only needs to be done once.

Horticultural sand

Horticultural sand (at least ⅛ in /3 mm in diameter) can be used to improve a poorly drained soil. Sand is heavy to move around so have it delivered.

Digging in horticultural sand

1 Aim to add a wheelbarrow full of sand for every 2–3 sq yd (2–3 sq m). Place in piles over the bed.

2 Dig the sand in well. Coarse sand will make an immediate and permanent improvement to the drainage of your soil.

DIGGING

Digging can be hard work, but it is extemely important to do if you have compacted or clay soils. Breaking up and turning the earth creates air spaces within the soil, making it easier for roots to penetrate the soil and grow. At the same time, you can bury any weeds that are present and add organic matter to improve the soil.

When digging topsoil, do not bring a lot of subsoil to the surface, as it lacks organic matter and is not fertile. Heavy clay soils are best dug at the beginning of winter. The exposed clods can be broken down by winter weather to a crumb-like texture, which is ideal for making seedbeds or planting in spring. Never dig or walk on the soil when it is wet and sticky: it may damage the soil. Lighter soils can be dug at any time but, as with all soils, leave at least one to two weeks after digging to allow the soil to settle before planting.

Single digging

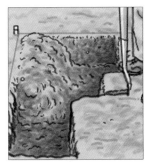

1 Dig out the first trench to one spade depth. Keep the spade straight and lift the soil out into a wheelbarrow or outside the area to be dug.

2 As you dig the second trench, this time put the soil into the first trench. Continue until the whole area has been dug. Use the soil from the first trench to fill the last trench.

Single digging is a very thorough method of digging an area. Remove any turf and divide the area into equal-sized trenches about 1 ft (30 cm) wide. Start in a corner and work standing on the next trench. The diagram below shows the correct order for digging.

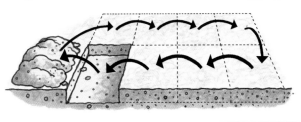

Feeding and Weeding

FERTILIZERS ARE PLANT foods. Unlike bulky soil improvers, which are added in generous amounts to improve the structure of the soil, fertilizers are concentrated, so apply them as directed on the packet.

There are three major nutrients required by plants: nitrogen, phosphorus, and potassium, often abbreviated to N, P, and K. Fertilizers that contain all three are known as general or compound fertilizers; they also often contain smaller quantities of trace elements. You can compare brands by looking on the fertilizer packets for the NPK figures. The percentage contained and the ratio between the nutrients is important. For example, an evenly balanced fertilizer promotes leafy growth, while a higher proportion of potassium encourages flowering and fruiting.

There are lots of brands of general or compound fertilizers available. Some, such as blood, fish, and bone, can be used all around the garden and tend to be the cheapest. Fertilizers for specific parts of the garden, such as lawns, roses, and containers, are expensive but are more convenient to use. For example, you can feed and weed your lawn in a single operation using a "weed and feed" preparation. Many container fertilizers include slow-release nitrogen, which needs to be applied once only at the beginning of the growing season.

Some gardeners prefer to use organic products, which are derived from either animal or vegetable sources. Both organic and inorganic products produce similar plant-growth results.

Applying fertilizers

Follow the manufacturer's instructions carefully. Wear gloves and wash your hands after each use. There is no need to dig in fertilizer as watering or rain will wash it into the soil. Dry fertilizer can scorch foliage, so brush it off or dilute with water. After applying dry fertilizer, water it to make it available to the plants.

ORGANIC FERTILIZERS

Fertilizer	Description	When to apply
Blood, fish, and bone	This is a powdery mixture of fast and slow-release nutrients. Use to promote general plant growth.	Apply in spring and through the growing season. It is difficult to apply in windy conditions.
Chicken pellets	These pellets provide fast- and slow-release nutrients. Use all around the garden for general plant growth.	Use in spring and throughout the growing season.
Seaweed meal	The slow-release nutrients and trace elements boost root and leaf growth.	Apply in spring.

INORGANIC FERTILIZERS

Fertilizer	Description	When to apply
Balanced general fertilizer	An all-round, fast-acting fertilizer with equal amounts of N, P, and K. Available as granules and as a liquid.	Apply in spring and throughout the growing season.
Lawn fertilizer	This fast-acting product promotes grass, leaf, and root growth. It is often sold combined with weedkiller.	Apply in spring and throughout the growing season. Some lawn fertilizers have different spring and fall formulations.
Rose fertilizer	A fast-acting product, high in K and trace elements. It promotes flowering in roses and other shrubs.	Use in spring and throughout the growing season.
Slow-release plugs	Fertilizer is held within a membrane that opens up and releases nutrients as the temperature rises.	Insert into compost in spring.
Tomato fertilizer	This fast-acting product is high in K. Promotes the growth of flowers and fruit.	Apply through the growing season. It is used for flowering and fruiting plants.

Weed control

A weed is any plant that you do not want. Weeds can make your garden look unattractive and they deprive your chosen plants of nutrients, light, and moisture.

Using weedkillers

Perennial weeds are difficult to control. Preparations containing glyphosate will help but several applications may be needed. For best results use before flowering. Many formulations are available, including ready-mixed spray guns and stick applicators. These are worth considering as you do not have to handle the chemical.

Path weedkillers can be applied with a watering can fitted with a dribble bar to distribute the liquid quickly and evenly. Use a can that is not used for watering plants. Weeds between paving slabs can be removed using a special weeder or a pen knife.

Lawns often need to be treated with commercial weedkillers (see page 75).

Hand weeding

Remove the whole root system and throw in the trash. Use a hoe to remove annual weeds. Hoeing is most effective when done on a warm, windy day, as the weeds dry out naturally on the soil surface. Annual weeds that have not flowered can be composted.

Weeding tools

A variety of inexpensive hand weeding tools is available for tackling weeds.

Onion hoe
For those who like to kneel down and hand weed small areas.

Handfork
Useful for digging out deep-rooted weeds in borders or vegetable plots.

Daisy grubber
Useful for lawns with a few large weeds.

Dutch hoe
For controlling annual weeds between plants.

Paving weeder
An alternative to using a path weedkiller on small areas of paving.

WEEDING TIPS

• *Do not leave bare patches of earth for weeds to colonize. Instead, use ground-cover plants or mulch well.*

• *Before planting, clear the plot of weeds. It is easier to weed unplanted ground than to weed between plants.*

• *Start weeding in early spring: weeds are easier to eradicate while they are young. Remove weeds before they seed.*

• *Weed regularly. Constant weeding when weeds reappear will eventually bring them under control.*

• *Dig out deep-rooted weeds. Try to remove as much of the root as possible.*

• *When using weedkillers, follow the instructions carefully and be prepared to reapply.*

Using a daisy grubber

Insert the narrow blade down near the root and pull it up. The weed, root and all, should come out without leaving a large hole.

Using a paving weeder

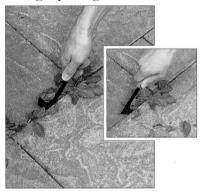

Push the weeder backwards and forwards in between slabs to sever the weeds. Inset: *Use the hook end to pull out the severed weeds. Put all the pieces of weed in the trash.*

Using a Dutch hoe

Annual weeds that grow between plants can be kept under control by regular hoeing. Use the hoe with a skimming action over the surface of the soil.

Mulching

MULCHING – COVERING the surface of the soil with an appropriate organic or inorganic material – prevents moisture from evaporating from the soil surface and, if applied correctly, prevents weeds from growing. Mulches are a boon for the weekend gardener as they can save you time on weeding and watering throughout the growing season. Mulches can be in the form of a loose material that is applied around established plants or a sheet that is put down before planting. Make sure that organic mulching material itself is free from any annual weeds.

The best time to apply a mulch is when the soil is warm and contains plenty of moisture. There is little point in applying a mulch in hot weather, when the soil is baked dry. One drawback of mulches is that if they are applied to cold soil, they act as an insulator; the soil remains cold, as the sun can't reach it, and this hinders plant growth. Loose organic mulches can dug in after about six months to improve the soil structure.

Ground clearing

Inorganic sheet mulches can also be used to clear a large, weed-infested area. Use any cheap material, such as old rugs or carpeting, plastic sheets, or lots of layers of newspaper, rather than a proprietary mulch.

Secure the sheets by digging a trench around them and then burying the edges (see opposite). Leave the sheets in place for a year, then remove them and dig the plot. This technique kills off even stubborn perennial weeds as it starves them of light.

Mulches

The factors to consider when choosing a mulch are cost, durability, and appearance. Inorganic mulches, such as sheets of plastic, can be used with a thin layer of loose, organic mulch to improve the appearance. Loose mulches should be at least 2 in (5 cm) deep to prevent weeds from growing through them.

Garden compost
This is free, but you will probably not be able to make enough. You can use shredded garden prunings and grass clippings but they may contain weed seeds.

Cocoa shell
A waste product from the chocolate industry. Ideal around smaller plants. It is expensive and not durable but it is attractive and pleasant to handle.

Gravel
Attractive as a path or for beds. Conserves moisture in soil but annual weeds may still appear. Various grades and colors are available – but the finer the grade, the greater the risk of cats using it as litter.

Woven polypropylene
Expensive but effective and durable. A heavy-duty material that can be used under paths.

Chipped bark
Easy to obtain, but look at samples before buying as quality varies. Aim for large chips of actual bark rather than wood. Expensive but attractive. The durability depends on the grade.

Floating row cover
Specifically made for mulching, so it is easy to handle and cut through. It is weedproof yet it allows in water and air. Expensive but effective.

Black plastic
Cheap and effective but harder to lay than commercial mulching materials. Durability depends on thickness.

Applying chipped-bark mulch

1 *Remove any weeds. Apply a general fertilizer to the soil, if necessary, and soak the ground if it is dry.*

2 *Next, apply a 2-in (5-cm) layer of chipped bark to the bare soil.*

Applying cocoa-shell mulch

1 *Remove any weeds and add fertilizer, if necessary. Water if the ground is dry.*

2 *Apply a 2-in (5-cm) layer of dry cocoa shells over bare ground. Water the mulch to bind it and prevent it from blowing away.*

LAYING A SHEET MULCH

Sheet mulches are easiest to lay on new beds or unplanted areas. They can be unattractive, but can be easily disguised, and are an excellent method of mulching a large area.

1 *Clear any weeds and complete the soil preparation then position the sheet. Lay a soaker hose under the sheet if watering is likely to be a problem.*

2 *Secure the edges of the sheet to hold it in place. Make a V-shaped trench with a spade and push the edges into the ground by hand.*

3 *Cut a cross with a sharp knife. Peel back the corners and dig out a hole in the ground underneath.*

4 *Insert the plant and push in firmly. It is important that the plant's roots make contact with the soil.*

5 *In an ornamental area, cover the sheet with an attractive loose mulch such as chipped bark. Commercial sheet mulch is expensive but durable.*

MULCHING TIPS

• *Mulch over the compost of container plants to conserve moisture. Cobbles and gravel look attractive in containers.*

• *When planting a specimen tree in a lawn, remove the surrounding turf as it will compete with the tree roots. Replace with a circular sheet mulch.*

• *To save money, recycle material from your garden to use in mulches. Grass clippings, shredded prunings, leafmold, and garden compost are all good materials to use as mulches.*

• *Buy mulching material in bulk to save money.*

Buying Plants

THERE HAVE BEEN SIGNIFICANT improvements in plant labeling and presentation over the last few years. However, buying plants can still be bewildering. To help, use the chart on pages 26–27.

Nowadays, most hardy plants are available all year as they are sold in pots or containers. This means they can be planted at any time of year as they have a rootball to support them. However, the easiest time to plant is in spring or fall as they will need less watering. The freshest stock is usually available in spring.

Plants are often sold bare rooted, which means they have been grown in a field rather than in pots. Bare-rooted plants are usually less expensive, but extra care is needed to protect the roots.

Flowering plants
When buying plants in flower, look for specimens with plenty of buds.

Buying good-quality plants
Most plants that have been recently delivered to garden centers are good quality and will establish well in your garden. Choose fresh plants that have plenty of young leaves or buds.

Plants with large foliage
Be sure that all the leaves are unblemished and intact.

Small pots
Plants in small pots dry out easily and need a lot of nutrients. Buy the freshest plants possible.

Bushy plants
Choose a stocky specimen that has lots of foliage and flowers.

Foliage color
Look for leaves that are a healthy color and avoid any that are mottled or have unnatural yellowing.

Plant names

Latin plant names are extremely useful for finding out more about the plant in reference books. There are two parts to a Latin name. The first tells you what genus (plant group) a plant belongs to. This, together with the second part, tells you the species; plants of the same species share most characteristics. If a non-Latin name in quotation marks follows, it indicates that this is a slight variation from the species. It may have been specially bred to produce a different flower color or to have a different habit. For example, *Thymus* ('thyme') *vulgaris* ('common') 'Silver Posie' (a specific variety).

TIPS FOR BUYING HEALTHY PLANTS

Where to buy
Buy plants from an outlet that has a high turnover: fresh stock is invariably more healthy than older stock. Department stores, DIY stores, and even petrol stations sell plants, but not all know how to look after them, or have the appropriate storage facilities. Retailers specializing in plants and gardening, such as garden centers and plant nurseries, do have that expertise and usually have a much wider range of plants for you to choose from.

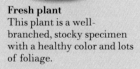

Fresh plant
This plant is a well-branched, stocky specimen with a healthy color and lots of foliage.

Older specimen
This tall, leggy plant has been on sale too long: note the roots on the surface and the poor shape.

Inspect the plant
Before you buy, always make a point of inspecting the plant carefully. There are five main things to look out for: plants that have plenty of new buds and shoots; well-branched, stocky specimens with a neat, overall shape; healthy roots; evidence that the plant has been correctly watered; and plants that are free of pests and diseases. See the column on the right for more information on how to check for these things.

Healthy leaves
The underside of the leaves should be free from pests.

Check the roots
Inspect the roots by tipping the plant out of its pot. Healthy roots of well-established plants hold the soil intact and lots of young roots – which are often creamy white – will be seen. If all the soil drops away, leaving a plant with small roots, this is a sign that the plant is not properly established. A potbound plant has a mass of dark brown roots growing around the sides and through the bottom of the pot, with little soil visible.

Healthy roots
Healthy roots that have filled out in the pot help the plant to get off to a good start in your garden.

Potbound plant
Roots growing through the bottom of the pot are the sign of a potbound plant. These will be harder to establish.

Check for signs of correct watering
Signs of underwatering are severe wilting, soil pulled away from the sides of the pot, and premature flowering. Overwatered plants could have damaged roots. Signs of overwatering are rotting foliage around the crown, gray mold, and smelly soil.

Check for pests and diseases
Crowded plants can become leggy and susceptible to pests and diseases. Avoid plants that have aphids on the leaves and the shoot tips. You should also avoid foliage that is distorted or twisted, gray mold on the top growth, any unnatural, mottled yellow foliage, fine webbing beneath the leaves, and loss of foliage (see pages 36–37).

Buying by mail order
Unpack the plants as soon they arrive. Contact the nursery at once if you find a problem. Try to plant bare-rooted plants immediately. If this is not possible because of bad weather, place them in pots of soil.

BUYING PLANTS (continued)

It is easy to allow yourself to be tempted into buying plants without any clear idea of where you are going to put them or whether they will look good together. Try to decide in advance what you want to buy. You may be copying a specific planting scheme, in which case simply take along a list with a note of how many plants of each species you need for your space. If you are not copying a specific planting scheme, consult a plant reference book. If you cannot decide in advance, note

down the size of the space you are trying to fill and consult the plant label before buying to check how tall the plant will grow and what its final spread will be.

Choose plants that are suitable for your garden. Note whether your site is sunny or shaded, and what the soil type is (see pages 14–15). If you have doubts about the suitability of a plant, consult the sales staff.

The following chart sets out the best time of year to buy the main types of plant and gives details of the forms in which you will find them.

GUIDE TO BUYING PLANTS

Plant type	When to buy	Description
Shrubs & trees	Available all year. The freshest stock is usually available in fall or spring.	Shrubs and trees are woody, permanent plants. Younger plants usually establish better and catch up with more expensive, larger specimens. Check the rootball carefully. Look for well-shaped plants with plenty of healthy foliage. Bare-rooted plants from mail-order nurseries are usually shipped from fall to spring.
Hedging plants	Available all year.	Pot-grown hedging plants are available from garden centers, but they are expensive. If you need a lot of hedging plants, buy bare-rooted plants from mail-order hedging specialists and plant in fall or spring.
Climbers	Available all year.	Most climbers are permanent plants sold in tall pots and trained to grow up a stake. Some, such as sweet peas, are annuals and can be bought as seed or young plants. If you are buying clematis, try to buy it when it is in flower, as it is often wrongly labeled and can only be correctly identified by its flowers.
Roses	Buy bare-rooted plants in fall. Container-grown plants should be bought from spring to summer.	Bare-rooted roses are generally inexpensive, but will not be in flower when purchased. Container-grown roses cost more. If you buy a container-grown rose, make sure that it has a full rootball.
Herbaceous perennials	Available all year, but the freshest stock is available in the spring and early summer.	These are nonwoody, permanent plants that grow above ground from spring to summer, with the top growth dying back during the winter. A few may be tender and need protecting from frost in some areas.
		Less expensive, small pots are available in spring, larger pots from late spring to summer. Fall is a good time to plant, but the top growth will have started to die down. Always check the roots and crown before you buy. Bare-rooted plants from mail-order nurseries are usually shipped from fall to spring.

Plant type	When to buy	Description
Annuals	Order from seed catalogs in winter or buy seed from shops or garden centers from winter to spring.	These are plants that flower and seed during the first year. They can be raised from seed or bought as plants (see bedding).
Bedding plants for summer color	Buy in spring or early summer.	These are temporary plants that remain in the garden for just one season. Some are tender perennials while others are half-hardy annuals, and they are often used in containers or beds. They can be bought at various stages of development from seedlings to more developed, pot-grown plants. You can buy plants or seeds by mail order or from garden centers. The more advanced the plant is when you buy it, the easier it is to look after. However, remember that you will pay extra for this. Do not plant tender plants until after the last frost in your area.
Bedding plants for spring color	Buy in fall or spring.	Similar to bedding plants for summer color (see above), but these plants are hardy, so they can be planted in the fall to provide a flowering display in the spring. After they have flowered, remove them to make way for summer bedding.
Bulbs for spring color	Buy as dry bulbs in fall and pot-grown plants in spring.	Dry bulbs can be bought loose or prepacked, but loose bulbs are easier to inspect for firmness and damage. Dry bulbs are relatively inexpensive but pot-grown bulbs are becoming increasingly popular as they will provide color more quickly. Snowdrops are often sold "in the green" — that is, as plants with green leaves that have already flowered. For conservation reasons, try to buy snowdrops that have not been collected from the wild. Most spring bulbs are permanent. Tulips are the exception, as they may last for only a few years.
Bulbs for summer color	Available as dry bulbs in spring and pot-grown plants in summer.	Similar to bulbs for spring color (see above), but many summer-flowering bulbs are not hardy so do not plant them until after the last frosts in your area. To keep them as permanent plants, lift them from the ground and store before the frosts start in fall.
Alpines	Available all year. The freshest stock is available in the spring.	These small, neat plants are ideal for rock gardens and are usually sold in small pots. Before buying, check that the soil is not over-wet and that the top of the plant is not rotten.

Sowing Seeds

IF YOU'RE A BEGINNER, sowing plants from seed might sound a little ambitious, but in fact it is remarkably simple. Follow the guidelines outlined on these two pages and you will never look back. You need only a small range of tools and materials (see below). Sowing from seed is also far less expensive than buying established plants – an important consideration if you have a large area to fill.

If you're not sure when to sow, or whether to sow under cover or outdoors, consult the seed packet; most come with clear sowing and raising instructions. However, if the weather is especially cold or wet, or if you have a heavy, clay soil, then it is worth raising seeds under cover even if the packet tells you that you can sow them outdoors.

Seeds in unopened foil packets last for several years, although the seed starts to deteriorate once the packet is opened. However, even an opened packet can be kept until the following year if you store it in an airtight container in a dry, cool place.

Tools and materials for growing seeds

You need only a few simple tools and materials to raise your own plants from seed. The basic items, shown below, are all inexpensive and easy to obtain.

Dibble
Use this small device for making holes in potting soil when preparing to transplant seedlings. You can improvize with the pointed end of a pencil.

Thermometer
Not essential, but useful for monitoring the temperature of your seeds. Many bedding plants germinate most rapidly between 60–65°F (15–18°C).

Potting soil
Use fresh potting soil that is weed-, fungi-, insect-, and disease-free. Garden soil is not suitable for seeds.

Labels
Label trays with the variety of seed and the date sown. Also include important germination instructions for later reference.

Mister
Use a plastic bottle with an adjustable nozzle to keep seeds moist without dislodging them. It can also be used to apply fungicide.

Vermiculite
These light and absorbent heat-treated particles of mica slowly release water and nutrients to seed starters. Add a thin layer over seeds that are sown on the surface of the potting soil.

Seed starter containers
Grow a single seedling in each cell to enable roots to grow with minimal disturbance. A peat-based soil is essential for small trays.

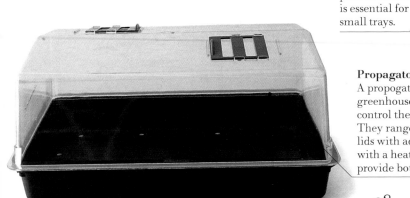

Propagator
A propagator is like a miniature greenhouse, allowing you to control the seed's environment. They range from ones with simple lids with adjustable vents, to those with a heater and thermostat to provide bottom heat.

Flat trays
Flat trays have a larger surface area of compost than round pots, so you can raise more seeds. They also fit into propagators more easily than round pots.

Sowing seed under cover

If you sow seed under cover, in a greenhouse, a propagator, or in the house, you will be able to exercise much more control over the growing conditions.

1 *Slightly overfill the seed tray with fresh, peat-based potting soil, breaking up compacted chunks, then level with a soil firming board. Stand the tray in water until the surface becomes moist.*

2 *To sow large seeds (shown above), hold them in the palm of one hand and space individual seeds on the soil surface. For small seeds, gently tap the packet to scatter the seeds evenly over the soil.*

3 *Using a flower pot or a sieve, cover the seeds with a thin layer of potting soil. If your seeds need light to germinate (the seed packet will give you this information), cover them with vermiculite.*

4 *Label the tray. Place it in a propagator or cover with glass or a clear plastic bag until the seedlings are large enough to handle. If the potting soil dries out, water from below or mist with warm water.*

TRANSPLANTING SEEDLINGS

When the first true leaves appear, thin out and transplant the seedlings into larger trays, or to other parts of the garden, to give them more space to grow. Handle seedlings by the leaves to avoid crushing the stem. (If a leaf is crushed, the seedling will still survive.)

Make a hole with a dibble or the tip of a pen or pencil, and ease the seedling in. Gently firm the soil around the seedling with your fingers. Water with warm water.

Hardening off

Seedlings raised under cover need to get used to outdoor conditions gradually before they can be planted outside – a process known as "hardening off," which takes 7–10 days. Place the plants in a closed cold frame – an unheated box with a hinged glass top. Open the lid during daylight hours, opening it wider each day until the plants adjust. Close the lid at night. Keep the seedlings watered. Add half the recommended amount of liquid fertilizer to the water. If you do not have a cold frame, set the plants outside on warm sunny days, increasing the amount of time you leave them outside each day. Bring them in at night. Later in the season, cover with a double layer of floating row cover at night.

Sowing seeds outdoors

Many hardy annual and perennial flowers, such as pot marigolds and night-scented stock, germinate so easily that it would be a waste of effort not to sow them outdoors, where you want them to flower; consult the seed packet for details. After sowing, keep the weeds down by hoeing and hand weeding. Thin the plants out when large enough to handle (see below left).

1 *First prepare a weed-free seed bed. Rake the soil so that it is level and has a crumbly texture.*

2 *Mark out the area you are planning to sow with light-colored sand or vermiculite.*

3 *Scratch out shallow lines with a stake, varying the angle from patch to patch. The lines should be 6–12 in (15–30 cm) apart depending on the plant. Consult the seed packet for details.*

4 *Water the soil before you sow if necessary. Sow thinly, taking a pinch of seed between thumb and forefinger. Cover the seeds with soil and firm down the soil.*

Planting

THE NEXT FOUR PAGES address the most common types of plant you are likely to encounter and show you step by step how to plant them. Before you plant, however, always clear the site of any weeds and add soil improvers if necessary (see pages 16–21).

Spacing is also important: almost all plants will grow to be considerably bigger than they were when you bought them. The plant label should tell you what the final height and spread are likely to be. Planting too close together makes extra work later as they can crowd each other out, while planting too far apart leaves space for weeds to colonize. This is less critical for annuals and summer bedding plants that only last for one season, as they do not spread far.

Planting equipment

For successful planting you will want to invest in a few multi-purpose, quality tools. The tools shown below are a good basic starting kit.

Hand fork
Use for weeding and cultivating the soil around established plants.

Trowel
Use for planting bedding plants and small perennials.

Bulb planter
This takes out a core of earth of uniform depth. Use for planting large numbers of bulbs or for planting bulbs in grass.

Spade
Use for digging planting holes for trees and shrubs.

Planting containers

Containers of all sizes are planted in the same way. Make sure water can drain away, so that the plants do not get waterlogged. Containers can dry out quickly, so incorporate water-retaining granules to reduce the amount of watering you need to do.

Although hanging baskets may look more complicated than other types of container, the principles of planting them are exactly the same (see page 62). A wide range of baskets and liners is available, but if you want to plant over the sides of a basket, opt for a traditional wire-mesh basket lined with sphagnum moss.

1 *Choose a container with drainage holes. Place a layer of pebbles or broken ceramic shards in the bottom to encourage drainage.*

2 *Add a layer of a suitable growing medium for your chosen plants. Crumble some slow-release fertilizer granules into the pot.*

3 *Prepare some water-retaining granules according to the instructions on the packet. Inset: Add the granules to the container and mix in to the potting soil.*

4 *Plant your largest plants first, laying a stake across the top of the pot to check that the plant is level. Add the rest of your plants, working outward from the center. Finally, water the container.*

Planting bulbs, tubers, and corms

Bulbs, tubers, and corms are dormant when you buy them. Plant them as soon as you buy them, or, if this is not possible, store in a cool, dry place. Most bulbs, tubers, and corms require a free-draining soil. If the soil is heavy, a shallow layer of fine gravel at the bottom of the hole will help to prevent them from rotting. If you want to keep tubers for several years, remove them and store over winter, then plant the following spring.

Planting bulbs in grass

To achieve a natural effect, plant bulbs randomly but at least one bulb width apart. Scatter large bulbs by hand and plant with a bulb planter. Plant smaller bulbs by lifting a section of turf.

1 Mow the grass to make planting easier. Scatter the bulbs randomly over the planting area.

2 Make a hole with a bulb planter. Inset: Plant a bulb with the pointed end upward, making sure it touches the soil.

3 Release the core of soil from the bulb planter. Press down the turf gently.

PLANTING DEPTHS FOR BULBS

Plant bulbs so that they are covered with two to three times their height of soil for optimum growth. Always check the instructions on the packet for precise planting details.

Soil level
4 in/10 cm
8 in/20 cm
12 in/30 cm

Daffodil   Hyacinth   Tulip   Snowdrop   Crocus

Planting water plants

Spring is the best time to add water plants to your pond. Floating plants, such as *Stratiotes aloides*, can simply be thrown into the water, as can oxygenating plants such as *Elodea canadensis*. Push marginal plants into the soft mud at the edge of the pond.

To plant true water plants, follow the instructions below. Any submerged leaves will soon grow to reach the surface of the water.

1 Line a special plastic water-plant container with burlap and half fill with soil. (The burlap prevents the soil from leaking out.) Inset: Carefully place the water plant in the container and gently firm around the stem.

2 Cover the surface of the pot with gravel to prevent the plant from floating to the top of the pond once it has been planted. Gently position the container on the bottom or, in a pre-formed pond, on a shelf at the side of the pond.

Planting bedding plants

A wide range of bedding plants can be bought from garden centers or by mail order. Harden your plants off in a cold frame for seven to ten days before planting them outside. Do not plant tender plants until the frosts are over in your area.

1 Allow the plants to soak in a shallow tray of water for about 20 minutes. Potting soil is prone to drying out as the pots are small.

2 Space out the plants in the border. Remove them from their pots or packs. Cut bedding strips into sections. Plant and firm the soil around the plants.

Planting ground-cover plants

Ground-cover plants are either perennials or shrubs and should be planted in the same way (see below and right). Make sure the beds are free from perennial weeds before planting as weeds are difficult to eradicate once the ground cover has become established.

Often a planting distance is suggested for a particular plant when you buy it. Close spacings provide quick cover, while wider spacings require fewer plants and so prove less expensive. However, remember that you will need to keep the ground between the plants weed free.

If you are using ivy as a ground-cover plant, make U-shaped pegs from 8-in (20-cm) lengths of galvanized wire and use them to pin the stems down to the ground at intervals. Cover the pegs with soil. The stems will root into the ground, giving you quicker cover.

Planting perennials

Perennials are often planted in groups of three or five, to create an impact. Buy several small plants or divide up larger ones. Plant bare-rooted perennials in the same way as bare-rooted shrubs (see right).

1 *Set the plants on the soil while they are still in their pots to check the planting distances and positions.*

2 *Water the plants, allow to drain, then plant at the same level they were in the pot.*

3 *Firm the plant into the soil so the roots are in contact with the soil. Water again if necessary. If slugs and snails are a problem in your garden, use a product containing aluminum sulphate to control them; traditional slug pellets are known to harm wildlife.*

Planting shrubs and hedging plants

When planting hedging plants or several shrubs in a border, be sure to allow them enough space to grow without crowding each other. Shrubs and hedges are easier to plant than trees (see right); there is no need to stake them and it is not normally necessary to install a hose for watering. As they have several stems, it is not critical to protect them from predators such as rabbits, but, if necesary, encircle the shrub with wire mesh.

1 *Turn over and weed the site. Set the plants at the correct planting distance. For hedging (shown here), stretch a taut string across the area to be sure you plant in a straight line.*

2 *Dig a hole for each plant. Check the spacing with a stake that you have cut to the correct planting distance.*

3 *Firm the ground around the base of each plant with your foot. Water thoroughly, directing the water to the base of the plant.*

TIPS FOR PLANTING BARE-ROOTED PLANTS

To protect the roots from drying out before planting, cover them with damp burlap. When you plant, spread the roots out evenly around the plant and make sure there is soil all around the roots. Bare-rooted deciduous plants should be planted in late fall, winter, or early spring — though not when the ground is frozen. Bare-rooted evergreens should be planted in mid spring.

Planting climbers and climbing roses

Soil at the base of a wall, tree, or hedge is likely to be impoverished, so when you are planting a climber or climbing rose always try to dig a hole at least 9 in (22.5 cm) away where the soil is more fertile and moist. If this is not possible, be sure to add plenty of soil improvers to the planting hole and mulch well to get the best out of your soil.

Plant climbers and climbing roses at an angle of about 45 degrees, so that they lean toward the support.

When you are planting climbing roses, always try to choose a fresh site in the garden. Soil that has had roses growing in it for several years can become "rose sick," so any new rose planted there is unlikely to thrive.

Planting trees

Trees, like shrubs, ground-cover plants, climbers, and hedging, are long-term plants and may need a little extra effort to get them established. Make sure the tree is well watered before you plant it and dig a sufficiently large planting hole to take the rootball. Mulching after planting will also help the tree to thrive without competition from other plants and weeds.

1 Remove a wide circle of turf. Dig a large hole to encourage new roots to spread. Add a handful of bone meal to the topsoil removed from the planting hole.

1 Dig a large hole at least 9 in (22.5 cm) away from the wall, shrub, or hedge. If you are planting a clematis, the hole should be about 6 in (15 cm) deeper than the pot in which you bought the plant. Add a soil improver (see pages 17–19) to the planting hole.

2 Plant the climber. Firm the soil around the base of the stem and water thoroughly.

2 Large trees need a stake to anchor them while the roots establish. Drive a stake into the ground at least 2 ft (60 cm) deeper than the bottom of the planting hole. Inset: Lay a pipe around the circumference of the planting hole with one end open at the surface so you can pour water directly onto the root ball.

3 Use a stake to guide the climber to the support. This could be a wooden trellis positioned against a wall or a host plant, such as a strong shrub or a tree. Secure the climber to the stake with string.

3 Remove the tree from its container and position it in the hole. Replace half the soil around the tree to steady it, then protect the tree with a plastic stem guard.

4 Replace the rest of the soil, firm down, and mulch. Inset: Attach the tree to the stake with a tree tie (a rubber belt with an adjustable buckle). Nail the belt to the stake to secure it.

Watering

WHEN WATERING YOUR GARDEN, concentrate your efforts on watering the plants that need it most. Make the task as easy as possible by planning ahead and investing in good equipment.

Soak beds or borders and lawns thoroughly once or twice a week. This is better than adding a little water every day. Light watering encourages the roots to grow around the surface of the soil rather than to grow down into the ground. Direct water at the plants' base. Water steadily, letting the soil absorb the water before you add more. If the flow is too fast, water will run off the plant, washing away soil and exposing surface roots.

Watering equipment

These are basic watering items that are essential in most gardens. There are many more items ranging from devices for watering growing bags to sophisticated irrigation systems.

Watering can
Many styles are available in metal or plastic, but those with a long spout and a detachable rose are the most versatile. Some come with a dribble bar attachment. Buy several watering cans in different colors if you need one for mixing chemicals.

Soaker hose
These are made from recycled rubber tyres. The sides leak water along the length of the hose. This is an easy way to water newly planted beds or hedging. Lay the hose on the soil surface around the plants or bury it in the ground.

Hose

Essential in all but the smallest garden. The easiest to use are those on a reel or a cassette. Many attachments are available. You can also buy devices for guiding the hose around corners without kinking.

Sprinkler
A hose attachment that sends droplets of water over a large area. Some types send out a static spray pattern; others oscillate or rotate the spray. A sprinkler can be used for watering lawns or beds. It can be wasteful: in hot weather much of the spray evaporates and in wind the spray is blown off target.

Easier watering

To save the time and effort of carrying water yourself, you can set up a watering system that moves water directly to your plants. Once it is set up, all you need to do is turn on the tap. Or, to ensure that your plants are watered regularly, you can install an electronic water timer that can be programmed to turn the water on and off for you at pre-set times. You can buy a complete kit or buy the components separately and design a system to suit your own garden.

There are various brands, but all work on the same principle. A supply tube (the diameter of a standard hose) has lengths of secondary tubing (micro tubing) inserted via adaptors at intervals along its length. The micro tubing, which is about $^{3}/_{16}$ in (4 mm) in diameter, takes water from the supply tube directly to each plant. A device that emits water is connected to the end of each length of micro tubing. Some devices cause a steady drip of water; others come out as a spray. Watering systems take time to set up and dismantle at the start and end of the growing season, but they save lots of time during the summer months.

Water barrel

Attach a downspout to your guttering, and direct rain water into a barrel where you can store it to use later for watering plants. Rain water is ideal for acid-loving plants but do not use it on young seedlings. Buy a barrel with a lid, to keep out dirt, and a tap. You may need to raise the water barrel so that a watering can fits easily underneath the tap.

WATERING HANGING BASKETS

Hanging baskets are often positioned above head height, which can make caring for them difficult. Also, because much of the growing matter is exposed, they may need watering up to twice a day in hot weather — although you can add water-retaining crystals to the basket to reduce moisture loss from the soil (see page 63).

Watering above head height

To make watering easier, attach a specially designed extender to your watering can or hose. You can also tie a stake to the end of your hose (as shown) to make the hose more rigid.

TIPS FOR WATERING

• *Make watering new plants, planted less than two years ago, a priority as their roots have not developed sufficiently to seek out water deep in the soil.*

• *Containers may need daily watering. Large containers do not dry out as quickly as small ones. Position pots in light shade during the the day.*

• *Herbs, mature trees, shrubs, and perennials should be able to cope during dry spells without watering. Lawns revive when it rains, so they are not a priority.*

• *Collect rain water in barrels. Use waste water, such as bath water, on older plants. Do not re-use greasy water.*

• *Insert a flower pot or hollow tube into the soil when planting specimen plants. You can pour water straight into the pot or tube to direct water to the plant roots. For beds of smaller plants, lay in a soaker hose.*

• *Young seedlings and plants in containers should be watered from below to prevent them from being dislodged.*

• *Reduce evaporation of water from the soil surface by applying a mulch in spring. Watering early in the morning or early evening, when the sun is low in the sky, also helps minimize evaporation.*

Pests and Diseases

PREVENTION OF A PROBLEM is always better than the cure. Good gardening practices, such as regular weeding, clearing away garden debris that may harbor pests and diseases, and keeping your plants watered and nourished, will do much to protect the health of your plants and to minimize the likelihood of problems arising. Encouraging natural predators, such as frogs, hedgehogs, birds, hoverflies, and ladybirds, into your garden will also help deal with many of the most common garden pests (aphids, slugs, and snails) in an ecologically friendly way. The other benefit of using natural predators is that you can avoid the overuse of environmentally harmful chemical controls.

If pests or diseases do occur, always deal with the problem as promptly as possible (see chart, below, for details of how to control some of the most common pests and diseases). Remove affected plant material as soon as you see the first signs of attack. Dispose of diseased material in the trash rather than on the compost heap to prevent the problem from spreading.

COMMON PESTS AND DISEASES: HOW TO PREVENT AND CONTROL THEM

Pest or disease	Symptom	Prevention and control
Aphids *Left:* Black fly (black aphid) on golden feverfew *(Tanacetum parthenium)*	Colonies of sap-sucking insects – often green or black. Usually found on young tips. There may also be a sticky honeydew and a black mold. Aphids are widespread and thrive in warm, sheltered conditions.	Encourage natural predators such as hoverflies and ladybirds. If aphids do appear, apply a contact insecticide: a systemic insecticide will work for about two weeks. Organic soap sprays are also available.
Caterpillars *Left:* Caterpillar of large white butterfly – *Pieris brassicae*	Petals and leaves eaten; caterpillars often seen inside flowers. Caterpillars thrive particularly in weedy, uncultivated ground.	Cover vulnerable plants with fine netting to prevent butterflies from laying their eggs. Pick off small infestations by hand or use a contact insecticide.
Slugs and snails *Left:* Slug on hosta leaf	Irregular holes eaten in the plant. Slime trails near the plant. Slugs and snails thrive in damp, shaded sites.	Put a ring of gravel or coarse sand around the base of young plants to prevent slugs and snails from reaching the stem, or scatter a product containing aluminum sulphate around young plants.
Whitefly *Left:* Whitefly and eggs on underside of leaf	Leaves are pale and sticky. Clouds of tiny white flies take off when the leaves are shaken.	Remove garden debris in the fall, since whitefly eggs may overwinter on leaves. Plant French marigolds near vulnerable plants. If whitefly do appear, use a suitable insecticide. Several applications may be needed.

Pest or disease	Symptom	Prevention and control
Downy mildew *Left:* Downy mildew on pea leaves	Leaves have yellow blotches and beige felt-like patches on the upper surface and grayish or purplish white patches of fluffy growth on the lower surface. Downy mildew is likely to occur in cool, humid places and when plants are crowded together.	If possible, plant varieties that are sold as being resistant to downy mildew. If downy mildew does occur, destroy affected leaves and spray with a suitable fungicide.
Damping off *Left:* Cress seedlings grown on infected (left) and healthy soil (right)	Seedlings collapse at soil level. The problem often starts in small patches of seedlings and then spreads. Damping off tends to occur in cool, moist conditions.	This is a soil- and water-borne fungus; using fresh compost and clean water can prevent the problem, as can spraying with a suitable fungicide. If it does occur, remove and destroy any collapsed seedlings.
Powdery mildew *Left:* Powdery mildew on *Rosa* 'Iceberg' buds and leaves	The upper surface of the leaves and shoots are covered in a white powder. Powdery mildew tends to occur in cool, humid conditions.	To prevent powdery mildew, keep plants well watered and avoid overcrowding. If it does occur, destroy affected leaves and spray with a systemic fungicide.
Rust *Left:* Rust on hypericum leaves	Symptoms vary but may include raised orange or brown spots on the lower leaf surface and stem. Rust tends to occur in humid conditions.	Prevent rust by improving air circulation around plants, and gathering up plant debris and weeds. If it does occur, destroy affected leaves or, if the whole plant is affected, dig up and burn. Spray remaining plants with systemic fungicide.
Viruses *Left:* Yellow stripe virus on *Narcissus* sp. leaves	Flecks or mottling on the leaves or flowers are usually a sign of a virus, although the patterns vary. The plant looks stunted or distorted. Viruses are carried by insect pests such as aphids.	Buy certified virus-free plants if they are available. Prevent viruses by controlling aphid attacks promptly, since aphids carry viruses. Viruses cannot be treated once they occur. Dig up and destroy the whole plant.

TIPS FOR PREVENTING PROBLEMS

• *Check the undersides of leaves and the growing tips of new plants for pests and diseases before you plant them.*

• *If a disease has been a problem in your garden, look for varieties that are resistant to specific diseases.*

• *Clear up plant debris, such as fallen leaves, weeds, and old pots. A neat, tidy garden offers fewer hiding places for pests than a weedy, badly tended one.*

• *Inspect young growth on plants regularly and take action promptly if there are any problems.*

• *The warm, humid conditions of a greenhouse are ideal for pests and diseases, so good hygiene and ventilation are especially important in greenhouses.*

• *Avoid overcrowding plants. Space them so that air can circulate between them and you can easily pick off dead foliage.*

• *Destroy infected plants by burning them or discarding them in the trash; never put them on the compost heap.*

• *Healthy plants are more likely to survive the onslaught of pests and diseases, so always carry out routine maintenance.*

Caring for Perennials

PERENNIALS DO NOT NEED to be replaced each year like bedding plants or hardy annuals. Once planted, they will come up year after year. How much maintenance they need depends on the species, although all need deadheading and cutting back each fall (see page 39).

Staking and supporting

Choosing perennials that do not need staking can save time, but most gardeners have a few favorite plants that they are prepared to go to the trouble of supporting in order to show off the flowers. Plants and trees that are over 1.2 m (4 ft) tall need to be staked for the first two years in order to support the plant. Stakes need to be in place by late spring, while the stems are still young and flexible and before the plant flowers. The plant should then grow through the staking system. The stake should not be visible once the tree or plant begins to flower. Supports are usually taken away in late fall, when the plants are cut back.

Stakes and supports

Various support systems are available. Factors to take into account are the cost and how visible the supports are on the plants. You should also make sure any sharp tips are covered to prevent people from injuring themselves.

Link stakes

These are L-shaped wires that can be joined together to form various types of support. Enclosed shapes, such as triangles, squares, and circles, can be made or the stakes can be linked in a line to hold back one side of a spreading plant from a lawn, path, or other plant.

Single stakes

One of the cheapest methods, particularly suitable for tall, large plants. Insert a circle of three or more stakes around the plant. Wrap string or twine around each stake in a circle.

Circular supports

These circular grids of metal or plastic are put over the top of low- or medium-height plants, such as delphiniums, to prevent them from flopping. The supports are held in place by metal legs or attached to supporting stakes.

Staking methods

The method you choose depends on the plant's strength and how you want to display it. Plants with woody stems need more support than soft-stemmed ones.

Stakes and string

1 *Insert 4 stakes into the ground in a circle around the plant, to a depth of 4–6 in (10–15 cm).*

2 *Wind string around each stake. Start near the bottom of the stakes. Repeat higher up as necessary.*

Link stakes

1 *Insert the longest end into the ground, join another stake on at the top, then insert into the ground.*

2 *Continue until a line of stakes has been formed. This will hold back a plant encroaching on a path or lawn.*

Circular supports

1 *Bend the rods into a circle and secure with a connector.*

2 *Adjust the position and size of the ring to suit the plant.*

Deadheading and cutting back

Remove dead flowers promptly. Although most perennials should be cut in late fall, they can be cut back in spring. Dead growth is ideal for the compost heap.

Plants requiring winter protection need a 6-in (15-cm) layer of insulation such as chipped bark or dead leaves. Remove insulation in spring or the plants may rot.

PROPAGATING PERENNIALS

Propagating is an economical and enjoyable way of increasing your existing plant stock and experimenting with new varieties.

Division

Plant roots can become crowded and deplete the soil. Rejuvenate perennials by dividing the whole plant and replanting the healthiest sections. This process can also be used to propagate more plants.

Divide plants in spring or fall when the plant is dormant. Lift out large clumps with fibrous roots first to allow you to divide the plant without trampling on neighboring plants. Smaller sections can be divided by hand. Split dense or woody plant crowns with a sharp spade or knife. Plants with rhizomes (underground stems) are easy to lift up from the soil. Cut into sections, making sure that each section has at least one shoot and some roots. Mature perennials only need to be divided every three to four years.

Cuttings

There are a variety of ways in which to take cuttings, depending on the season and the maturity of the plant, but usually softwood cuttings, taken in late spring or early summer, are the most successful. If this method does not work, use the same technique to take semiripe cuttings in late summer.

Rooted geranium cutting
A softwood cutting (see below) was taken in spring.

1 *Cut 3 in (7.5 cm) off a strong, young shoot with a sharp knife. Remove lower leaves and dip stem in hormone rooting powder or liquid.*

2 *Plant the cutting in potting soil and water. Cover the pot with thin plastic wrap and put in a shaded cold frame.*

Pruning

ANY TREES AND SHRUBS do not need regular pruning, just an occasional cutting back to keep them under control. Plants trained into formal shapes, such as wall shrubs or hedges, also need regular pruning to maintain their shape. There are a few exceptions that benefit from annual pruning; check the plant label whenever you buy new plants.

Whatever shrubs you have, always remove dead or diseased branches that can spread to the rest of the plant. You can distinguish the dead wood from live wood by scratching the stem with your thumbnail. If green-colored wood is exposed, then the stem is still alive; if it is brown or white, then the stem is dead.

Knowing whether your shrubs flower best on old wood or on new will help you decide the best time to prune. Old wood is usually darker with a rougher surface, and new wood is lighter and smoother. Once a stem has flowered, cut it back to allow room for replacement flowering stems to develop the following year. Remember, always feed the plant after pruning to encourage new growth. Mulch in spring after the weather has warmed up.

Pruning tools

Most pruning can be done with pruning shears. Large hedges, however, may require shears or a hedgetrimmer. For more mature trees and shrubs, with branches large than ³⁄₈ in (1 cm) in diameter, you need one or more of the following tools. Take into account the height and accessibility of your trees and shrubs when choosing tools.

Hedge shears
Ideal for new or small hedges, topiary, and low-growing shrubs such as heathers. The blades need to be kept sharp and adjusted so that they cut efficiently.

Pruning shears
An essential garden tool. Keep the blades sharp; it is worth buying a brand that offers replacement blades. Check that the handles are comfortable and the safety catch is easy to use.

Loppers
Ideal for cutting branches up to 1¹⁄₈ in (3 cm) in diameter. The long handles make it easier to reach into prickly or congested shrubs. Some models are heavier than others, so handle a few before buying.

Hedgetrimmer
The longer the blade, the quicker you can cut. Gas-powered models may be best for a large garden. Electric trimmers are less expensive, lighter, and quieter. Battery-powered versions are also worth considering. Choose a model with plenty of safety features.

Pruning saw
A useful tool for branches over 1 in (2.5 cm). The arrow tip makes it easy to cut between branches. Choose a model that can be folded up when not in use.

Shredder
A shredder is worth considering if your garden produces a lot of tree and shrub prunings. Shredded prunings can be used as mulch or added to a compost heap. This is kinder to the environment than burning them. Shredders are expensive to buy and need to be stored safely. You will need protection from the noise as well as gloves and eye protection. Choose a model that offers safety features and can be moved around easily.

Bow saw
A fast way to cut thick branches and logs. Replacement blades are available.

Making the right cut

Make clean cuts with sharp blades. A blunt blade means you have to pull and twist to make a cut, which causes damage to the plant tissue. The angle of the cuts depends on how the buds are arranged on the stem. Most stems have alternate buds (see below). Make a sloping cut just above a bud so that any rain will run away from it. This will reduce the risk of a water-born infection. For opposite buds, cut straight across.

Alternate buds
For a plant that has alternate buds (buds that are placed alternately up the shoot), prune with a diagonal cut just above an outward-facing bud, as shown.

Opposite buds
For a plant that has opposite buds, prune with a straight cut across the stem directly above the buds.

When to prune

Pruning in winter produces vigorous growth the next season as the plant's energy is directed to fewer buds. Pruning in summer removes leaves that produce the plant's food, thereby slowing down growth. Pruning in the later summer or fall can stimulate fresh growth that may be vulnerable in frosty weather, so it is usually not recommended (although tall, shallow-rooted plants, such as rambling roses, are an exception, since they can be damaged by high winds).

Generally, winter or early spring is the time to prune plants that flower in late summer, whereas plants that flower in spring or early summer should be pruned once their flowers have faded. Try to prune at the right time – but if you are in doubt, remember that pruning at the wrong time of year is unlikely to do irrevocable damage to the plant.

Pruning overgrown shrubs

Pruning is essential if your shrubs are overgrown. This applies to both deciduous and evergreen shrubs.) Stagger the reshaping of overgrown shrubs over a three-year period to minimize shock to the plant. In the first year, cut out one stem in three after the shrub has flowered. (If the shrub flowers after mid-summer, do not prune until early the following spring.)

Cut out old or sickly stems or badly placed branches. Leave the shrub alone for a year to produce new growth. In the second and third years, tackle the remaining old growth. You will need loppers and a pruning saw (see opposite) to prune mature shrubs.

Young shoots
Old shoots

Stagger the pruning of overgrown shrubs
Remove one third of the old stems after flowering in the first year. Trim remaining old growth in the next two years.

Pruning deciduous shrubs

Shrubs that flower in late summer usually flower on wood made earlier in the season. Prune in winter or early spring to give plants time to make new wood. Cut back the stems of vigorous plants, such as *Buddleia davidii*, to within two buds of last year's wood. Remove only stems that have flowered and older growth on vigorous shrubs, such as *Hydrangea microphylla*.

Deciduous shrubs that flower in early or mid-spring or early summer should be pruned immediately after flowering to give them as much time as possible to produce flower-bearing wood for the next year. Remove the stems that have just flowered, cutting them back to the previous year's wood. With shrubs that flower when new woody growth has started, be careful not to remove newly grown stems that have not yet flowered.

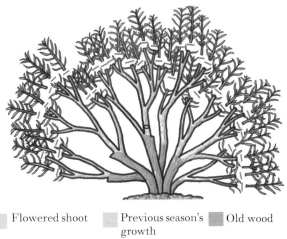

Flowered shoot   Previous season's   Old wood
                  growth
Pruning early-flowering deciduous shrubs
Prune just after flowering so that the plant has maximum time to make flower-bearing wood.

41

Some deciduous shrubs are grown not for their flowers but for some other attractive feature. Dogwoods and willows, for example, are grown for their colorful, bare winter stems. Cut these plants back each year to encourage a flush of fresh, young growth. Some plants, such as lilac, can be grown for their attractive leaves. Cut these back to ground level each spring to create an attractive, leafy summer shrub.

Pruning evergreen shrubs

Most large evergreen shrubs need no regular pruning. If they get straggly, treat them in the same way as any overgrown shrub (see page 41) and reshape them over a three-year period. Some evergreens, such as aucuba and eucalyptus, however, are extremely resilient and respond well to being cut back drastically, so there is no need to stagger their renovation.

There are many small evergreen flowering shrubs, including many useful ground-cover plants and herbs, that need to be clipped annually. Lavender, cotton lavender, periwinkle, marjoram, and thyme all fall into this category. Some plants, such as lavender, dislike being cut back too far into old wood, so trim off their flowers and 1–2 in (2.5–5 cm) of the foliage each spring. Cotton lavender can be deadheaded after flowering in summer; in spring, cut far back to within 3–6 in (7.5–15 cm) of the ground, just as the new shoots start to develop, to keep the plant compact. Clip other ground-cover plants to keep them dense and bushy.

Pruning to maintain shape
Pruning shrubs, such as cotton lavender, will encourage new growth and help the plant to keep a regular shape.

Pruning climbing and rambling roses

With climbing roses, training the rose sideways along horizontal supports is more important than actual pruning. Rambler roses produce more growth from the base than climbers, so they can become untidy if not properly trained. Both rambling and climbing roses should be deadheaded regularly throughout the flowering season. Cut back the stems to the next set of leaves beneath the dead flower.

Rambling roses

Mature ramblers should be pruned in late summer after flowering. Cut back any old, diseased, or weak shoots to ground level using loppers. Cut side shoots to leave around three healthy buds or shoots. Tie all the young shoots to secure.

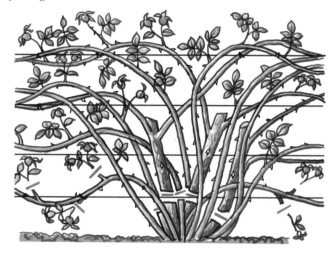

Pruning rambling roses
Cut back stems that have flowered to the supporting stems of the plant in late summer or fall. Use loppers or a saw to reduce the framework if the plant needs to be thinned out.

Climbing roses

Train these regularly so that you catch them while the growth is still flexible. Remove any dead, diseased, or weak growth in late fall after flowering or by early spring. Reduce side shoots to 4–6 in (10–15 cm) at the same time. Roses trained along chains or rope between poles may need to have some of the old shoots cut out to keep the plant under control.

Pruning climbing roses
Prune in late fall or early spring if they need to be restricted to a particular space. Cut back side shoots to 2–3 buds or 4–6 in (10–15 cm). Cut back the stems to a healthy bud.

Pruning wall shrubs

Shrubs that are trained against walls require annual pruning and training to keep them manageable. Put up a means of support, such as a trellis or horizontal wires (see pages 103 and 107), and plant the shrub about 9 in (23 cm) from the wall.

Firethorn (Pyracantha)

In the early years, tie leading stems to the wires with twine or wire ties. Once the framework has formed, you will need to prune annually. Shorten new side shoots in mid-summer so that only two or three leaves remain on each one. If you do not get around to summer pruning, the plant can be tidied up in late winter by clipping with shears. Cut back any extra-long shoots at the same time.

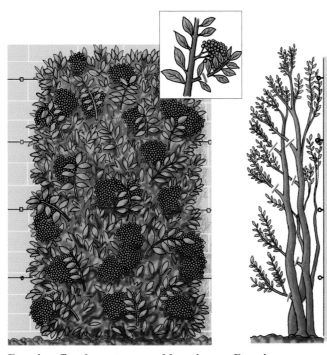

Pruning firethorn to reveal berries
To prevent firethorn berries from being hidden behind new shoots, cut back the new shoots once the flower buds or berries are visible. This will also encourage flowers and berries to grow in subsequent years.

Pruning firethorn to tidy overall shape
Cut off surplus branches that are growing away from the wall.

Pruning climbers

Some varieties of climber are extremely vigorous and can take over the garden if left untended. If pruned regularly, they are ideal for adding interest and height, and can be used to disguise unattractive walls or fences or screen an overlooked part of the garden.

Wisteria

These are very vigorous climbers. After the initial training, which takes three years, prune each summer and winter. In mid to late summer, cut back the extension growths to within five or six leaves or 6 in (15 cm) from the main stem. In winter cut back the same growths again to 2–3 buds or 3–4 in (7.5–10 cm).

Late summer
Trim back long side shoots to within 6 in (15 cm) of the main stem.

Winter
Cut back side shoots to within 3–4 in (7.5–10 cm) of the main stem.

Honeysuckle

Climbing honeysuckles are divided into two pruning groups depending on when they flower. The first group includes those that flower on the current season's growth, such as the Japanese honeysuckle and its varieties. Cut back the whole plant in early spring. Passion flower can also be pruned by this method.

The second group includes honeysuckless such as *Lonicera periclymenum* that flower on the previous season's growth. They can be left unpruned, but to tidy them, cut back each flowered shoot to a point where there is a young shoot to replace it.

Clematis

There are three pruning groups depending on flowering time and vigor. Not all need pruning, but group 3 requires regular pruning to flower well.

Group 1

Group 1 comprises evergreen and early, small-flowering species and varieties. Prune after flowering if the plant is untidy. Group 1 clematis include:
Clematis alpina *and cultivars*
Clematis armandii *and cultivars*
Clematis cirrhosa *and cultivars*
Clematis macropetala *and cultivars*
Clematis montana *and cultivars*

Group 2

Group 2 comprises large-flowered species and varieties that flower from early summer. Cut back the healthy stems by one third in early spring, before flowering. Cut to a pair of strong, healthy buds. Group 2 clematis include:
Clematis *'Barbara Jackman'*
Clematis *'Lasurstern'*
Clematis *'Marie Boisselot'*
Clematis *'Nelly Moser'*
Clematis *'Niobe'*
Clematis *'The President'*

Group 3

Group 3 clematis flower during late summer. In early spring, cut away all the previous season's growth to about 30 in (75 cm) above soil level. Group 3 clematis include:
Clematis tangutica *and cultivars*
Clematis viticella *and cultivars*
Clematis *'Hagley Hybrid'*
Clematis *'Jackmanii'*
Clematis *'Perle d'Azur'*
Clematis *'Ville de Lyon'*

Pruning hedges

Hedges need regular pruning, but wait until after birds have left their nests. Most hedges can be trimmed with shears or a hedgetrimmer, but hedges with large leaves should be finished with pruning shears. To save time, use pruning shears only for the most visible areas.

Keep hedges low and narrow to save time. Most hedges can be lowered if they have grown too large but stagger the work over a couple of seasons. Lay a sheet of plastic along the length of the hedge before you start cutting to speed up gathering fallen clippings.

Tall, formal hedges should taper at the top. This saves cutting time and means that the bottom growth is not shaded, so the hedge should have foliage all over. Low-growing hedging does not need to taper.

PRUNING HEDGES

Hedge	When to cut	Pruning tips
Beech (*Fagus sylvatica*)	Mid-summer	Prune with shears to prevent cut leaves from turning brown.
Box, dwarf box (*Buxus sempervirens*)	Mid-summer	Can be clipped far back making it a useful subject for topiary.
Lawson's cypress (*Chamaecyparis lawsoniana*)	Mid-summer	Do not cut back into old wood; leave 4 in (10 cm) of live foliage.
Leyland cypress (*Cupressocyparis leylandii*)	Mid-summer	Do not let it reach more than 7 ft (2 m) high.
Holly (*Ilex*)	Mid-summer	Prune with shears to prevent cut leaves from turning brown.
Lavender (*Lavandula*)	Mid-summer	Clip lightly with shears after flowering.
Privet (*Ligustrum*)	Late spring to mid-summer	Clip each month through the growing season.
Yew (*Taxus baccata*)	Spring or late summer to early fall	It will regrow even if cut far back into old wood.
Western red cedar (*Thuja plicata*)	Mid-summer	It will sometimes regrow but not always if you cut back into old wood.

Pruning to remove problem areas

Even trees and shrubs that do not need regular pruning should always have dead, diseased, or problem branches removed as quickly as possible.

Frost damage
Young growing tips of evergreens are often caught by the frost or by cold, dry winds. Cut back to healthy wood once the danger of frost has passed.

Diseased wood
Diseases can gain entry via damaged tissue. Cut back to healthy wood just above a bud. Do not put diseased prunings on a compost heap; always burn them or put in the trash.

Damaged wood
Cut back to undamaged wood before the tissue becomes infected.

Crossing branches
Crossing branches make the plant look unattractive and the friction caused by two branches rubbing can damage them. Remove the weakest branch or the one that spoils the shape.

Weak, spindly branches
Cut back weak branches harder than strong, vigorous stems to encourage a more balanced growth.

Suckers
These unwanted shoots grow up from the base of the plant. Scrape back the soil until you find the origin of the sucker, then pull or cut it off close to the main stem.

Variegated plants
Sometimes these produce all-green shoots that are more vigorous than the rest of the plant. If these are not cut out they will take over the whole plant.

SAFETY

• *Wear suitable protection, such as goggles and heavy-duty gloves, when pruning. When using an electric hedgetrimmer, work with the cable over your shoulder.*

• *Pruning mature trees requires great care if you have to work overhead or from a ladder. In most instances, it is safer to call in an arborist to tackle medium and large trees.*

• *Always close the blades of the pruning shears after use and store safely.*

Making a New Border

A NEW FLOWER BED or border can transform your garden. The keys to success are careful planning and site preparation. Before you plant anything, take the opportunity to prepare and condition the ground thoroughly. This may be the only time that you have access to completely bare soil, so it is worth going all out to improve your soil and give your precious new plants the best possible start. This is particularly important for permanent plants, such as trees and shrubs.

Planning your border

First, measure your site and make a drawing of the area on squared paper, using a scale of about one square to 12 in (30 cm). This enables you to plan the dimensions and shape of your border with more confidence. Once you have the basic shape on paper, lay tracing paper over the top and experiment with different shaped borders, such as long thin ones or deep sweeping curved ones. It is often a good idea to add some paving slabs to create a visually firm edge – especially when a border goes around a corner. Think about bed maintenance, too – a paving slab path laid at the back of a deep bed will quickly disappear behind your plants but can make weeding and pruning easier.

Plan before you plant
Once you have settled on a plan, mock it up before you start digging to check that the plan works in practice.

As well as any paving, mark on your plan the position of large plants, such as trees, shrubs, or large herbaceous perennials. Every border should have at least one major plant, often more than one. These plants will provide the basic framework to your planting and you should position them so that they are clearly visible from your home and other parts of the garden.

What works on paper doesn't always work so well in real life, so mock up your plan, and if necessary adjust the posistions of the plants. Lay any paving slabs (see opposite) for edging paths or maintenance access before you begin to dig your new bed.

Preparing the site

Remove the turf from the site and dig the soil to one spade's depth. If necessary, prepare a maintenance path (see opposite). Break up large clods of earth with a fork, and add a multi-purpose fertilizer. Ideally do this in the fall, for planting the following spring.

1 *Mark out the border with a line of garden stakes and wind twine around them to give you a clear line to follow. Alternatively, you could lay a hose on the ground as a guideline. Inset: If you are cutting a new border out of an existing lawn area, as here, cut out the shape with a half-moon edging tool and then use a spade to lift the turf.*

2 *If you are putting in a maintenance path (see box opposite), position the slabs. This is to enable you to check the approximate positions before you start digging: there is no need to dig and improve soil that is going to be covered by paving slabs. If necessary, redistribute earth beneath the slabs to get a level surface.*

3 *Dig the border with a fork to one spades' depth, putting plenty of compost or manure in the bottom of each successive trench (see page 19).*

Planting the border

Once you have planned out the border, prepared the ground, and bought your plants, you can position and plant them. Work from the back of the border to the front to save treading on the soil. Plant the largest specimens first, remembering to dig a generous planting hole and add fertilizer to the roots. Then plant the medium-sized shrubs and perennials and finally the smaller, front-of-the-border perennials.

1 Position the feature plants in their proposed planting positions. If you are happy with these, dig the planting holes, adding fertilizer, and plant them one by one, firming the soil around each plant with your foot. Remember to stake any tall-stemmed trees.

2 Continue to work round the border from the back (or in this case the two sides) to the front. It is a good idea when planting container grown plants to tease the rootball out, as here, before planting, in order to ensure the roots get away to a good start.

TIPS FOR PLANTING A BORDER

• *To create natural-looking clumps of herbaceous perennials, plant groups of three, five, or seven plants. Even numbers of plants tend to look more orderly and less natural than odd numbers.*

• *If all the tall plants are at the back of a border, the planting can look over-formal. Stagger the planting line, so that the tallest plants are not all in a row.*

• *As a general rule, plant combinations of contrasting shapes, alternating upright and spiky plants with rounded and bushy ones.*

EDGING PATH

In practice, you would lay a maintenance or edging path at the same time as preparing the site. It is shown separately here, as it is not an essential part of all beds and borders: it is a good idea if your border is wide, as you can gain access to your plants to carry out any garden maintenance, but it is not essential. Without a path you would have to trample on the soil and risk damaging the soil structure and the plants.

Edging paths get relatively little use, so they do not need to be concreted into position. Make sure the ground is level before you put down any paving slabs – otherwise they may not be stable.

Level the ground and check with spirit level. Remove any stones and rake smooth. Lay a 1-in (2.5-cm) thick layer of coarse sand as a bed for the slabs. You can brush sand between the slabs to create a grout into which small plants will seed themselves, creating a more natural effect.

1 Level off the soil and lay the sand bed. Position the slabs in place, ensuring each slab is level by laying a spirit level across it, and tap down using a large mallet.

2 Continue to position the slabs until they are all in place and level. Brush sharp sand between the slabs to create a grout.

3 The edging path provides a working area from which to tend the planted border.

The Weekend Gardener's Calendar

THIS CALENDAR SETS out what you need to do to maintain your garden throughout the year. As a weekend gardener, the best way to maximize your time and keep your garden in good condition is to carry out routine tasks, such as weeding or mowing the lawn, each weekend. If you keep on top of things you'll be able to complete these essential jobs quickly.

The tasks will vary depending on what plants you have chosen to grow. Therefore only general guidelines are given here, providing a season-by-season, page-at-a-glance reminder of what you need to do and when. For specific information on particular plants, refer to a plant reference manual and to the maintenance tips that accompany each project in this book.

The exact timing of routine garden maintenance is rarely critical; it's impossible to give precise timings as conditions vary so much from one part of the country to another. Weather conditions vary, too – not just from one part of the country to another, but also from year to year. Your best key to success is to learn a little about how plants grow and the conditions that they need in order to thrive; once you understand the requirements of your plants, you will find it easy to gauge the right time to prune a particular shrub, for example. Even if you do prune your plant at the "wrong" time of year, you are unlikely to cause irrevocable damage: you may simply have fewer flowers the following year.

Use the weekend gardener's calendar as a prompt – don't become a slave to it. Instead, relax and enjoy doing what tasks you can when you have the time: that's what weekends are for!

SPRING

Containers

• Plant new containers, but wait until the danger of frost has passed if you are planning to use frost-tender plants.

• Keep the soil in containers moist, especially when they are newly planted.

• Keep frost-tender container plants inside in a sunny spot until the danger of frost has passed, so that they will be well developed when they are ready to go outside. Harden them off gradually (see page 29), leaving them outside a little longer each day.

• For permanent container plants, discard any winter frost protection and remove dead or unwanted growth from the plants. Scrape off the top 2 in (5 cm) of potting soil and replace it with fresh, incorporating some slow-release fertilizer granules.

• As the weather warms up, watch out for diseases and pests, such as aphids (see pages 36–37), and deal with any problems immediately.

• Check hanging basket and window box brackets to make sure that they are still securely fixed and in good condition.

Lawns

• Lay or sow new lawns (see pages 74–77).

• Start mowing established lawns as soon as the grass is visibly growing. Remove any debris from the lawn before you mow using a fan-shaped wire rake. Maintain the grass between ½–2 in (1–5 cm) long.

• Trim the lawn edges when you mow with a weed whacker or long-handled shears.

• Remove clippings, since dead grass clippings can build up thatches of dead material on the surface of the turf.

• Repair any broken lawn edges, bumps, or dips (see page 77).

• Remove large, tap-rooted lawn weeds, such as dandelions, using a daisy grubber or narrow trowel or small hand-fork (see page 77). Fill any holes with lump-free soil and a little grass seed and cover the patch with hay or chicken wire to protect the seed and seedlings. Alternatively, rather than handweeding, use a selective weedkiller and fertilizer formulation, following the manufacturer's instructions for dose and application.

Annuals and Bedding Plants

• Sow hardy annuals where they are to flower or in pots or trays indoors (see page 29).

• When the seedlings of fall-sown hardy annuals are large enough to handle, transplant them to where you want them to flower (see page 29).

• Keep frost-tender and half-hardy bedding plants indoors until the danger of frost is over (see page 31).

• Pinch out the tips of sweet-pea seedlings to create multistemmed climbers; pinch out side shoots to create taller ones.

Perennial Plants

• In late spring to early summer, take softwood cuttings from tender perennials such as geraniums (see page 39).

• Cut back and discard any dead growth that was left on perennial plants over the winter.

• Lift and divide over-large clumps of perennials not divided in fall (see page 39).

• Position supports for tall perennials while the plants are small (see pages 38–39).

Trees, Shrubs, and Climbers

• Trim low hedges, using hand shears rather than an electric trimmer to avoid bruising the leaves.

• Check that the stakes used to support any climbing plants are firm and sound.

• Tie stray stems of climbers.

• Remove any dead, diseased, or broken stems.

• In early spring, prune shrubs that flower after mid-summer, if necessary (see page 41), feeding them with slow-release fertilizer granules after pruning. Small, summer-flowering evergreen shrubs, such as lavender and cotton lavender, should be pruned each year to keep the plants compact (see page 42).

• In early spring, trim hedges that are planted with summer-flowering climbers such as clematis.

• Cut back shrubs, such as dogwood, that are grown for their colorful winter stems once their leaves begin to emerge.

• Prune spring-flowering shrubs immediately when flowers fade (see page 41).

• Plant bare-rooted deciduous trees or shrubs before the leaves emerge. Plant bare-rooted evergreen shrubs in mid-spring (see page 32). Container-grown shrubs can be planted at any time during the year, though not when it is frosty or when the soil is very wet (see pages 32–33).

Herb Gardens

• Sow seeds of annual herbs such as parsley.

• Cut out individual straggly stems of large woody herbs such as rosemary and sage.

• Clip small, bushy herbs, such as thyme and marjoram, to keep the plants compact.

Wildflower Gardens

• If you have a spring-flowering meadow, do not mow it during spring. Instead, make a note of where different spring-flowering wild species might be encouraged to grow next year.

• Weed over-vigorous plants that threaten to shade their neighbors.

Woodland Gardens

• Avoid pruning or clipping plants that might support nesting birds.

Water Gardens

• Remove any plants that have outgrown their planting baskets. Divide them and repot in fresh soil.

• Add more water to the pond if necessary.

• Plant new water plants and marginals in the late spring (see page 31).

• Make sure the soil in the bog garden is moist. When the soil has warmed, in mid-spring, add a layer of compost or manure around the base of the plants as a mulch.

• Use a fan-shaped wire rake to scoop out algae and debris from ponds.

General Maintenance

• Thoroughly weed beds and borders (see pages 20–21). If you do this job well, before the weather warms up, your plants will grow quickly to overwhelm weeds.

• Make sure the ground around the base of your trees, shrubs, and climbers is kept clear of weeds and grass.

• Once the soil has warmed, cover exposed, weeded ground with a 2–3-in (5–7.5-cm) layer of mulch (see page 22-23).

• Mulch around the base of trees, shrubs, and climbers in late spring once the soil has warmed up, giving the plants a thorough watering first if the soil is dry.

• Plant the new beds that you prepared in the fall (see pages 46–47).

• Check that trellises, walls, and fences are sound. Repaint if necessary.

• Watch out for infestations of aphids on new growth. Spray with soapy water or remove and dispose of badly infected stems.

• Water plants – particularly newly planted ones – if the weather is warm and dry.

• Sweep paths and paving with a stiff broom. Apply handfuls of coarse sand to the path before sweeping to help remove any slime.

• Lift any rocky paving slabs, add coarse sand underneath to correct the rocking, and tamp down the slab, checking that it is level with the others.

• Remove any weeds that are growing between paving slabs (see page 21).

SUMMER

Containers

• Finish hardening off frost-tender seedlings and plants (see page 29), then plant them.

• Keep all containers watered (see pages 34–35). If you are going to be away from home for a weekend, move the containers close together in a shaded position and thoroughly soak them. If you are going to be away from home on a regular basis, or for longer than one weekend, ask a neighbor or friend to water your plants – or consider a installing an automatic watering system.

• Remove spent flowers to encourage new flower growth.

• Snip off any dead leaves: they look unsightly and may harbor pests and diseases.

• Remove weeds regularly.

• In early and mid-summer, add liquid fertilizer to the water (use the manufacturer's recommended dosage).

Lawns

• Mow regularly while the grass is growing (unless you are creating a meadow). Keep the grass to a height of about ½ – 2 in (1–5 cm). (You can leave it as long as 2 in/5 cm in hot weather.)

• If you have naturalized bulbs in your lawn, do not mow until the leaves have shrivelled.

• Trim the lawn edges when you mow with a weed whacker or long-handled shears.

• If you have left an area of lawn to develop into a spring-flowering meadow, use a weed-whacker to cut the grasses and flowers once they have seeded themselves. Leave the cuttings to dry, then rake them up.

• Remove weeds that are shading out grasses using a narrow-bladed trowel or a daisy grubber.

• For a dense, healthy turf with no wild flowers, use a general-purpose lawn feed (see page 75).

Annuals and Bedding Plants
• Snip off dead and tired growth regularly to make way for fresh leaves and flowers.

Perennial Plants
• Watch out for slugs and snails and set traps for them if necessary (see page 36). Large bites taken from leaves and a silvery trail will alert you to the problem.

• In mid-summer, take cuttings of tender perennials, such as pelargoniums, to grow on for next year (see page 39).

• If you have an over-large clump of iris, lift and divide it once the flowers are over.

Trees, Shrubs, and Climbers
• Prune late spring- and early summer-flowering shrubs and climbers that flower before mid-summer (see pages 41–44).

• Prune trained trees and shrubs. Pruning at this time of year discourages growth, making it easier to keep the shape that you want (see page 43).

• Clip hedges and topiary 1–3 times during the summer months, using sharp shears or pruning shears.

• Dead head roses and other shrubs to encourage more flowers to grow.

• Tie climbers as they grow up or along their supports.

• Loosen any tree ties that have become too tight for the tree.

• Shorten the side shoots of young non-flowering wisteria plants to encourage flowering.

Herb Gardens
• Snip off or pinch out flowering stems of herbs as they appear, since herbs are generally thought to taste better before they flower.

• Clip shaped bay trees to keep their growth dense and their shape neat.

• Clip small, bushy herbs, such as thyme and marjoram, to keep them compact.

Wildflower Gardens
• Once spring meadow flowers have faded and seeded, cut

them down. Leave cuttings to dry, then add them to the compost heap.

Water Gardens
• Add water to the pond, as necessary, to maintain the desired water depth.

• Snip or pull off any water lily leaves that are pushing out of the water.

• Remove pond weed or algae as it appears, scooping it out with a fan-shaped wire rake or twirling it around a stick.

• Keep the soil in the bog garden moist and well weeded.

General Maintenance
• Water plants regularly during hot weather. Water the plants in the shade as the water will evaporate quickly in sunlight and may cause scorching. It is particularly important to water newly planted plants, as their root systems have not yet established. More established plants will also benefit from a thorough soaking.

• Weed regularly. If weeds grow through a mulch, pull out and top up the mulch.

• Remove dead flower heads as they appear to encourage more flowers.

• Weed gravel paths and paved areas regularly.

• Add more gravel to paths if necessary.

• Sweep decking paths to keep them clean and non-slippery, and remove any weeds.

• Watch for infestations of aphids on new plant growth. Spray with soapy water or remove and dispose of badly infected stems.

FALL
Containers
• Plant pots of spring-flowering bulbs (see page 31 for planting depths) – or use a trowel or bulb planter to plant them in established pots.

• Drain off excess rain water so that your pots don't become waterlogged.

• Lift and remove frost-tender perennials from outdoor containers, pot them, and bring in to a frost-free place.

Annuals
• Sow hardy annuals for early flowers the following year. Sow them where they are to flower or in pots or trays and keep them in a sheltered place, such as a cold frame, during the winter. Thin out the seedlings when they are large enough to handle.

• Discard annual flowers once they no longer look attractive.

Perennials
• Cut back dead fern fronds. Use dead fronds to insulate vulnerable plants in winter.

• Lift and divide any over-large clumps of perennials.

• Plant winter- and spring-flowering bulbs in bold groups around the garden, especially in places that can be seen from the house (see page 31 for planting depths).

Trees, Shrubs, and Climbers

•Fall is the best time of year to plant your new trees and shrubs, while the soil is still warm and there is time for roots to begin to grow before the cold weather sets in.

•Prune rambling roses once flowering is over (see page 42). Other roses, unless they are in an exposed position, are best left until spring.

Lawns

•Sow lawn seed or lay new turf now, before the winter, or wait until spring.

•Carry out any repairs to your lawn while the grass is still growing (see page 77).

•Rake up leaves from the lawn (use them to make leaf mold or compost).

•Replace lost air from compacted soil in a lawn by spiking the lawn with a garden fork in boggy areas to introduce air into the soil under the turf. Push the fork in vertically to a depth of 4–6 in (10–15 cm), then withdraw it vertically. Take care to avoid levering the fork, as this will uproot the turf.

•Add a top dressing of equal parts of sieved sand, soil, and peat; rake half a bucketful per square yard (meter) over the lawn surface. This will help to nourish the turf and fill minor bumps and hollows.

•Continue to mow the lawn while the grass is still growing, but raise the height of the blades so that you don't cut the grass any shorter than about ¾ in (2 cm).

•Plant drifts of spring-flowering bulbs in areas of your lawn to create a natural-looking effect (see page 31).

Herb Gardens

•Cut back mint. Lift and divide mint plants that are overcrowded.

•Tidy beds of herbs and mulch using compost or farmyard manure.

Water Gardens

•Remove any frost-tender water plants and store them in buckets of water in a frost-free place.

General Garden Maintenance

•Tidy beds and borders. Remove unsightly dead growth – but remember that some plants can look attractive as they die off in fall so don't cut back everything. Leave any new growth at the base of the plant.

•Fall is the best time to improve the soil in your garden (see pages 16–19).

•Design and create new beds (see page 46–47).

•Apply a 2-3-in (5–7.5-cm) layer of a coarse mulch, such as bark chippings, to the surface of the soil between the plants and around trees, shrubs and climbers before the cold weather, since this will help to insulate the soil (see pages 22–23).

WINTER

Containers

•Stop watering plants in containers.

•Discard dead plants and store their pots for next year.

•Stand containers in a sheltered spot for the winter. If they are left to stand in the rain, freezing rainwater may crack the container and damage the plants' roots. Drain off rain water so that remaining plants are kept relatively dry in cold weather.

•Protect vulnerable plants that you keep permanently in containers by bringing them inside (into an unheated room) or by wrapping them in straw (or dead fern fronds) and tying plastic sheeting around the plants.

•Clean containers by scrubbing them in soapy water with a little disinfectant.

Perennials

•Fleshy-rooted plants are more vulnerable to frost damage than fibrous-rooted ones. Perennials with a "crown" of leaves are also at risk, since rain can trickle into the plant and rot it. Protect vulnerable perennials by covering them with straw, dead fern fronds, or prunings from evergreens.

Trees, Shrubs, and Climbers

•Knock heavy falls of snow off branches since they can snap under the weight and disfigure the plant.

•Prune the side shoots of wisteria back to within 3 in (7.5 cm) of the main framework of the plant.

•Between winter and early spring, prune late summer-flowering shrubs such as buddleia. As a general principle, prune in winter, when plants are naturally dormant, rather than in fall. Fall pruning can encourage new growth, which may be subjected to frosts.

Lawns

•Avoid walking on lawns during cold, wet weather since you can easily damage the soil structure and therefore soil fertility.

•Clean and sharpen lawn tools; wipe the blades with an oily cloth before storing them in a dry shed or cupboard.

Water Gardens

•Clean the pond pump filter.

•If you have fish in your pond, make sure there is always a hole in the ice during freezing weather.

General Garden Maintenance

•Firm soil down around plants where it has been lifted by frost.

•Make sure that paths and paving are swept regularly and kept free of ice.

•Buy seed catalogs and plan what you are going to plant next year.

CONTAINERS

Potted profusion
This varied collection of pots makes an impressive display of colors and textures against the plain background of the evergreen hedge. The spiny, sword-like clumps of variegated century plants (Agave americana 'Variegata') provide a distinct, almost architectural, structure to this profusion of pink and white geraniums, lilies, and other blooms. What better solution is there for a dull front yard than a vibrant blend of foliage and flowers?

Ideas for Using Containers

WHATEVER KIND OF outdoor space you have – large or small, a city apartment or a country home – containers of plants can create an almost instant garden. In this respect, containers are ideal for the weekend gardener: quick to plant and relatively easy to maintain. You can find a style to suit any situation, too, from rustic-looking wooden half barrels and terracotta troughs to elegant Versailles tubs that would grace the most sophisticated mansion.

Containers are also a great way of making your gardening more flexible. You can move them around to vary your view. You can grow frost-sensitive plants and bring them inside when the weather turns cold. You can use a different type of soil to the one that is naturally found in your garden – enabling you, for example, to grow acid-loving plants, such as camellias and azaleas, even if your garden soil is alkaline. And you can celebrate each season by replacing spring-flowering bulbs with summer bedding.

The questions on these two pages are designed to help you pinpoint ways in which you can use containers to enhance your garden. Each one is backed up by a step-by-step project that includes suggestions for container plants to use in your own garden.

? *Do you have large expanses of bare paving?*

Visually, containers of plants help to soften an expanse of paving or other hard surface, and add color and interest where beds cannot be created. *Right:* Even this small patio would look bare and uninviting without potted plants to soften edges and break up straight lines. Here, pots of purple pansies with lime-green flowering tobacco plants add a splash of color, while the clipped box and the ivy cones give the patio a sense of fun. SEE *Grouping Pots, page 56.*

? *Does the entrance to your home look untidy?*

Well-tended containers next to the front door create a wonderful first impression for visitors and make the whole house seem loved and cared for. SEE *Brightening up a Doorway, page 58.*

❓ Do your walls or window ledges need brightening up?

Containers are a quick-and-easy way of adding color and interest. *Left* : Scarlet trailing geraniums and purple flowering lobelia bring vibrant color to the front of this house throughout the summer. The variegated hebe in the window box and spotted laurel in the troughs provide this planting with attractive foliage.

SEE *Hanging Baskets, page 62;*
Window Dressing, page 64;
Brightening Bare Walls, page 66.

❓ Is your garden too small for a pond?

Even if your space is restricted, you can still make an interesting water feature in a container. *Left:* In this trio of barrels, potted ivy, ferns, and mosses create a tiny, lush water garden.

SEE *Water Feature for a Small Space, page 68.*

❓ Is there a view or feature that you want to hide?

Containers of estabished plants are ideal for instantly blocking an unwanted view and enhancing your privacy.

SEE *Screening with Containers,*
page 60.

Grouping Pots
CONTAINERS FOR PATIOS

CONTAINERS ARE A GREAT WAY OF softening the hard expanse of a patio area and adding color, but unless it's large and imposing, a single pot can look stark and isolated. You can create a stronger visual effect by arranging several containers together. Moreover, grouping pots means that the display is less exposed than it would be if the pots were arranged singly – and some of the plants will benefit from being slightly more sheltered.

When deciding how to group pots, decide whether you want a formal design or a more relaxed style. For a formal, consciously stylish arrangement, choose a matching set of pots and a simple, clearly coordinated planting – a row of potted white lilies behind pots of lavender in matching but smaller containers, for example. An informal, more accessible approach would be to vary pot styles, shapes, and materials and also the plants you put in them, although some linking theme – flower color or leaf texture, pot material or glaze, for example – should be apparent to hold the arrangement of pots and plants together visually.

When it comes to choosing plants, a useful rule of thumb is that tall, upright containers need something to trail down them and soften the outline of the pot, while rounded containers generally need an upright and bushy plant as a contrast in shape.

Informal grouping for sun

This trio of pots, two made from glazed terracotta and one left plain, makes an attractive grouping. Although they are different in color, size, and shape, the fact that they are all made from the same material gives them unity. The choice of plants, too, helps to unify the display: lady's mantle appears in two of the pots and, although they are somewhat smaller, the nasturtium and New Zealand burr leaves are sufficiently similar in shape and texture to the lady's mantle for them to work well together. The running bamboo provides much-needed height and a contrast of texture, while the nasturtium flowers give a splash of color that is echoed by the flowers of the New Zealand burr.

1 Running bamboo
(*Pleioblastus auricomus*)

2 New Zealand burr
(*Acaena microphylla*)

PLANTING ALTERNATIVES

Formal partners for shade

For a shaded patio area, choose plants that thrive in such conditions. The hosta and fern shown below are ideal partners: their leaves contrast in shape and texture, and the mottled green and yellow hosta will reflect what light there is. If space is tight, create a display with height by placing a tall container inside another one; this way the base of the taller pot is softened and it doesn't look so stark. Here, two wooden planters have been put together with a hosta in the taller planter, and a delicate-looking fern at its base.

1 *Hosta fortunei* var. *albopicta*

2 *Polystichum setiferum*

Polystichum setiferum

Hosta fortunei var. albopicta

PROJECT PLANNER

TIME SCALE **1 HOUR**

Tools and Materials

Containers • Broken ceramic shards • Trowel • Potting soil • Slow-release fertilizer granules • Water-retaining granules

1 *Clean old pots or buy new ones. Be sure to wash out any old soil. Dry pots thoroughly.*

2 *Experiment with different arrangements of the empty pots to work out how you will group them. If you are using three pots of different shapes and sizes, a triangular arrangement often works well.*

3 *Calculate roughly how many plants you will need for each group and buy them. If you cannot plant them immediately, keep them watered and in the shade.*

4 *Plant the containers (see page 30). Water thoroughly and allow to drain.*

5 *Wash or wipe off any mud on the outside of the container or around the rim.*

6 *Position the containers in the arrangement you have chosen. Make sure pots are on level ground.*

MAINTENANCE

• *Keep the pots watered and weeded.*

• *In the fall, plant a few spring-flowering bulbs, such as crocus, to add interest early in the year.*

• *In spring, scrape away the top inch (2 cm) or so of soil and replace it with fresh.*

• *Keep the plants tidy. Snip off any dead foliage or flowers once they've faded. Cut back over-vigorous growth.*

• *Remove the nasturtium in the fall once it begins to look untidy. Plant fresh nasturtium plants the following spring once the frosts are over.*

3 Lady's mantle (*Alchemilla mollis*)

4 Nasturtium (*Tropaeolum majus*)

Brightening up a Doorway
CONTAINERS FOR A SUNNY SITE

CONTAINERS OF flowering plants next to the front door create a wonderfully welcoming atmosphere for visitors and are the perfect solution for paved areas or steps where you cannot plant directly into the ground. Large containers make a dramatic impression and are easier to care for, since they contain more soil and moisture than small ones.

Doorway containers need to look good all year round, so include some permanent plants (ivy, wisteria, and cotton lavender are used in this design). After the frosts have passed, introduce summer bedding plants. In the fall, remove the bedding plants and plant spring- and winter-flowering bulbs. For instructions on how to plant a container, see page 30.

1 Geranium (*Pelargonium* 'Clorinda')

2 *Petunia* 'Super Cascade Lilac'

3 Ivy (*Hedera helix* 'Gracilis')

4 *Wisteria sinensis*

5 Cotton lavender (*Santolina chamaecyparissus*)

6 Night-scented stock (*Matthiola bicornis*)

Sunny lilac and yellow pots

This lilac and yellow planting is suitable for a sunny site. The wisteria will need support and also pruning in summer and winter if it is to flower profusely and be kept to a manageable size. However, its early summer blooms and beautiful foliage make the effort well worthwhile. The geranium and petunias give a continuous show from early summer until the fall. Cotton lavender, with its gray foliage and yellow flowers, brings a contrast in color to the other plants, and ivies trail over both pots to soften their edges and help to marry the two very different-looking containers. In the fall, plant some winter- and spring-flowering bulbs.

PLANTING ALTERNATIVES

Shady glow

Substitute the shade-loving plants listed below for those illustrated (left). A pink and white fuschia replaces the geranium, with a busy Lizzie providing a splash of lilac. The ivy will thrive in shade and sun. A Japanese aralia replaces the wisteria. Golden-green variegated euonymus replaces cotton lavender and a tobacco plant provides a strong scent.

1 Fuchsia 'Mary Poppins'

2 Busy Lizzie (*Impatiens* 'Super Elfin Pearl')

4 Japanese aralia (*Fatsia japonica*)

5 *Euonymus fortunei* 'Emerald 'n' Gold'

6 Tobacco plant (*Nicotiana alata* 'Lime Green')

PROJECT PLANNER

TIME SCALE 1+ HOURS

Tools and Materials

Wires and vine eyes • Containers • Gravel • Potting soil • Water-retaining granules • Slow-release fertilizer granules • Trowel

1 *Put up wire supports on the house wall (see page 103) to give the wisteria something to cling to as it grows.*

2 *Buy the plants. If you cannot plant them immediately, store them in a cool place and keep well watered.*

3 *Position the containers. Fill the bottom of each container with gravel and top with 12–18 in (30–45 cm) of potting soil, mixing in water-retaining granules and fertilizer granules following the manufacturer's instructions.*

4 *Plant the wisteria (with its supporting stake) first; undo any ties that are holding the plant to the stake and replace with wire ties or loosely tied soft twine. Set the plant at a slight angle so that it slopes backward and its cane leads the plant back to the wall. (You can remove the stake after a year or so, once the wisteria is firmly attached to the wire supports.) Plant the remaining plants (see page 30) and water thoroughly.*

MAINTENANCE

• *Deadhead flowers once they are past their best.*

• *Water daily. Six weeks after planting, add liquid feed to the water, following manufacturer's recommendations.*

• *Lift and remove geraniums and petunias in the late fall, before the frosts set in. You can take cuttings of geraniums in the late summer or early fall. Alternatively, overwinter geraniums in a frost-free place.*

• *Plant winter- and spring-flowering bulbs in place of the geraniums and petunias to keep the containers looking fresh and colorful.*

• *Once the basic shape of the wisteria is established, prune back the side branches to 3 in (7.5 cm) of the main stem each winter. In summer, trim any long, straggly side shoots to about 6 in (15 cm) in length and tie the wisteria to the wires as it grows.*

• *Clip cotton lavender after it has flowered.*

Screening with Containers
TROUGH WITH CLIMBING ROSES

ALMOST EVERY GARDEN has a small area, such as a compost heap or garbage cans, that would be better hidden from view. For a quick-and-easy solution, place a trough backed with a trellis in front of the unsightly object, and plant it with climbers and bushy evergreen shrubs. The plants will soon provide a dense screen and make an attractive feature.

If you need to move the screen from time to time – in order to gain access to a drain, for example, or to clear away fallen leaves – screw wheels under the trough so that it can be pushed out of the way when necessary.

For extra summer color, add bedding plants such as the yellow petunia shown below. In the fall, plant spring-flowering bulbs such as crocuses or dwarf tulips.

Sunny screening

This planter has plenty to distract you from the view beyond – especially in the summer, when you use the garden most. The trellis is adorned with ivy, giving all-year cover, while the rose bears yellow blooms throughout the summer.

2 Yellow climbing rose (*Rosa* 'Golden Showers')

3 Jerusalem sage (*Phlomis fruticosa*)

1 White variegated ivy (*Hedera helix* 'Glacier')

4 *Petunia* 'Yellow Pearl' (yellow multiflora type)

MAINTENANCE

- *Water frequently, twice daily in dry weather.*

- *Six weeks after planting, add a liquid fertilizer to the water once a week until midsummer, following the manufacturer's usage recommendations.*

- *Fix the climbers to the trellis as they grow.*

- *Deadhead the roses as they pass their best to encourage more flowers.*

- *In the fall, lift and discard the petunias. Remove the top 1–2 in (2.5–5 cm) of potting soil and replace with fresh soil. Plant winter- and spring-flowering bulbs.*

- *Cut back any dead or unwanted growth of the Jerusalem sage and the climbers in spring.*

PLANTING ALTERNATIVES

Shady site

If your trough is in a lightly shaded position, substitute the following plants for those illustrated. Ivy thrives in sun and shade, but change the rose for a firethorn and enjoy flowers in spring and colorful berries in the fall. Exchange Jerusalem sage for a white-flowering hebe, an evergreen that will tolerate less than ideal light conditions. Busy Lizzies replace the petunias at the front of the trough, but do not plant them until the frosts are over.

2 Firethorn (*Pyracantha* 'Orange Glow')

3 *Hebe albicans*

4 Busy Lizzie (*Impatiens* 'Super Elfin')

PROJECT PLANNER

TIME SCALE 1/2 DAY

Tools and Materials

Planter, at least 12 in (30 cm) deep • 2 posts of 3 x 3 in (7.5 x 7.5 cm) pressure-treated wood about 3 in (7.5 cm) taller than the trellis panel • Screws and screwdriver • 2 decorative post caps • Spirit level • Pencil • Trellis panel approx. 6 in (15 cm) narrower than the planter • Four 2-in (5-cm) trellis brackets • Four 2-in (5-cm) castors • Wood sealant • Plastic sheet • Broken ceramic shards • Potting soil • Water-retaining granules • Slow-release fertilizer granules • Trowel

1 *Position one post on each side of the back of the planter, checking that you have left enough room for the trellis panel. The posts should extend beyond the bottom of the planter so that they rest just above the ground after the castors have been fixed in place (see step 5). Attach the posts, using two screws each in order to secure, and fix a decorative post cap to the top of each post.*

2 *Holding the trellis panel in place, use a pencil to mark the position of the brackets near the top and bottom of the side posts.*

3 *Screw the brackets to the trellis and side posts.*

4 *Set the castors in place on the base of the trough and mark the position of the screws. Screw on the castors.*

5 *Apply a coat of plant-friendly wood sealant. This protects the wood and helps to harmonize the coloration of the posts, trellis, and trough.*

6 *Cut holes in a plastic sheet and line the trough with it. Put in ceramic shards, potting soil, water-retaining granules, and slow-release fertilizer granules.*

7 *Buy the plants. If you cannot plant them immediately, store them in a cool place and keep them well watered.*

8 *Plant the rose and ivy at the back of the trough, entwining the stems through the trellis. Plant the Jerusalem sage and petunias at the front. Water thoroughly.*

Hanging Baskets
SEASONAL COLOR

NOT ALL PLANTING needs to be at ground level. Extend your garden upwards by means of an eye-catching display of hanging baskets and wall pots (see also pages 66–67).

The critical thing to remember with hanging baskets is that, because they're normally positioned at eye level or higher, the base will be seen as much, if not more, than the top and sides. Bear this in mind when you're planting: no matter how eye-catching the top may be, nothing can ruin the effect more than a dried-out, colorless covering of moss along the sides and bottom.

Don't include too many colors. You can create just as dramatic an effect with just one or two toning shades: delicate blue and white, perhaps; or even, for a shaded alleyway, a monochromatic collection of shade-loving foliage plants such as ferns.

The only special requirements for hanging baskets are regular watering – potting soil dries out quickly in a small container like this – and a sturdy, securely fixed wall or ceiling bracket. Hanging baskets are quite heavy, particularly just after watering, so any bracket must be strong and secure enough to bear the weight.

Pastel shades for summer
This selection of advancing warm-colored and receding cool-colored pastel shades gives an impression of a great depth of planting. The flowers are all of a similar size, so no one element dominates the display.

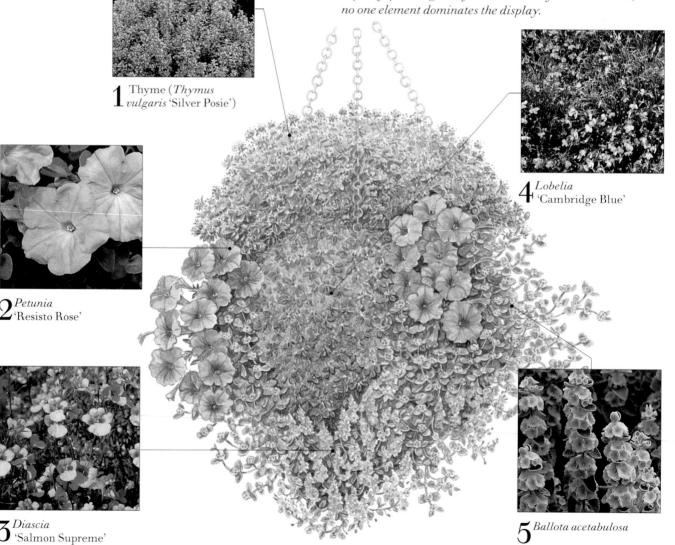

1 Thyme (*Thymus vulgaris* 'Silver Posie')

2 *Petunia* 'Resisto Rose'

3 *Diascia* 'Salmon Supreme'

4 *Lobelia* 'Cambridge Blue'

5 *Ballota acetabulosa*

MAINTENANCE

• *Water the basket regularly, especially in warm dry weather. To make watering easier, keep a step stool nearby or fit a special lance-like attachment to your hose (see page 35).*

• *Snip off any unwanted straggly growth and dead flowers as soon as they appear so that the basket maintains its neat overall shape.*

• *Apply a liquid feed regularly, following the instructions supplied by the feed manufacturer.*

• *Every year, and especially after stormy weather, check that the brackets are still secure.*

PLANTING ALTERNATIVES

Pastel shades for winter

For an attractive winter hanging basket in a pink and white color scheme, replace the plants shown in the design opposite with the following:

1 Heather (*Erica* sp. – many varieties available)

2 Variegated ivy (*Hedera* sp. – many varieties available)

3 *Cyclamen coum*

4 Snowdrop (*Galanthus nivalis*)

5 White winter-flowering pansy (*Viola* sp. – many varieties available)

PROJECT PLANNER

TIME SCALE 1 HOUR

Tools and Materials

Wall bracket and screws • Drill and appropriate bit • Wire basket • Flower pot • Sphagnum moss • Black plastic • Scissors • Potting soil • Slow-release fertilizer granules • Water-retaining granules

1 Attach a bracket or hook to the wall to hang your basket from and check that it is secure. Buy the plants. If you cannot plant them immediately, store in a cool place and keep well watered.

3 Line the moss with black plastic trimmed to fit the basket. Make slits all around the plastic at intervals of about 3–4 in (7.5–10 cm).

2 Balance the basket on a flower pot or bucket at a convenient working height. Line the basket with a generous layer of damp sphagnum moss.

4 In a bucket, mix fresh potting soil with slow-release fertilizer granules, following the manufacturer's instructions.

5 The first plants to go in, around the side and toward the bottom of the basket, are the trailers. Water them first, then gently push their rootballs through the holes in the basket and plastic, past the sphagnum moss.

6 Place some water-retaining granules at the bottom of the basket (follow the instructions given on the packet for amounts). As you add more plants and soil, mix in more granules.

7 At the top, use an upright, bushy plant in the center surrounded by spreading plants and more trailers. Top with soil, leaving the finished level 1 in (2.5 cm) below the rim. Hang the chains that are attached to the basket from the hook or bracket that you put on the wall in Step 1.

Window Dressing
WINDOW BOX FOR SEASONAL COLOR

WINDOW BOXES are an easy way of brightening up an empty window ledge and making your home look well loved and welcoming. Choose plants of different habits – some upright, some trailing – and plant them close together to give an impression of luxuriant growth. Contrasts of color are important, too, and the planting below uses a classic combination of scarlet and green to great effect.

Window boxes need regular watering – at least once a day in hot weather. If they are not easily accessible, install an automated watering system (see page 35).

The climate on a window ledge can be extreme – from baking sun to howling winds – so it is wise to replant every season and stick to robust species that can withstand these conditions and give you a long period of color. Geraniums, petunias, and lobelia are some all-time favorite window-box species.

A plant-filled and well-watered window box can be extremely heavy, so it needs to be securely fixed in place. If you have window ledges for your boxes to sit on, use wedge-shaped blocks of wood under the box to make sure that it is perfectly level. If possible, attach chains to the sides of your box and hang on hooks that you can screw into the outside wall. If you don't have window ledges you can still put up boxes, but they will need wall-mounted brackets to rest on (see opposite).

Strong colors for summer

The scarlet geraniums shown here will flower all summer long with little attention and contrast boldly with the neat, clipped box cones. The ground ivy and helichrysum trail over the edge of the container to provide a contrast in shape with the more upright forms of the box cones and geraniums. The box cones can stay in the window box permanently as long as they are in good condition. They help to give the arrangement structure, and provide a solid green backdrop for the other plants.

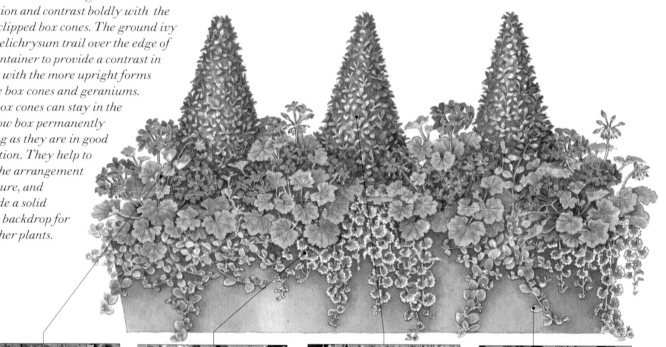

1 Geranium (*Pelargonium* 'Madame Fournier')

2 Ground ivy (*Glechoma hederacea* 'Variegata')

3 Box (*Buxus sempervirens*)

4 *Helichrysum petiolare*

MAINTENANCE

• *Water thoroughly – at least once a day in hot weather.*

• *Add a liquid feed to the water six weeks after planting, then once each week, following the manufacturer's instructions.*

• *Snip off any unwanted growth or dead flowers as they appear. Clip box cones to keep their shape.*

• *Watch out for aphids. Cut out and dispose of badly infected stems.*

• *Take cuttings of frost-tender plants in late summer or fall (see page 39). Remove them from their container before the frosts and overwinter in a frost-free place.*

• *Every year, and especially after stormy weather, check that the brackets are still secure.*

PLANTING ALTERNATIVES

Silvery shades for winter

In the fall you may need to replant your window box with frost-hardy subjects. If you are leaving the container in position, plant bulbs in pots so that they can be easily lifted and replaced when their flowers are over. Choose early and late winter-flowering bulbs to keep a continuous display through to spring.

1 Snowdrop
(*Galanthus nivalis*)

2 Winter iris
(*Iris unguicularis*)

4 Silver variegated ivy
(*Hedera helix* 'Heise')

PROJECT PLANNER

TIME SCALE 1/2 DAY

Tools and Materials

Window box • Two window box brackets • Spirit level • Drill and masonry bit • Screws and screwdriver • Anchors • Liner to fit window box • Broken ceramic shards • Potting soil • Water-retaining granules • Slow-release fertilizer granules • Trowel

1 *Hold the window box in place to determine where you want to attach it. Be sure that the location you choose will give you a good view of the plants while not preventing you from opening the window.*

2 *If you do not have a window ledge, fit brackets to support the window box. Mark the screw holes for each bracket, using a spirit level to check that the bracket is straight.*

3 *Use a masonry drill bit to make screw holes in the wall. Inset: Push an anchor into each screw hole.*

4 *Push the screw through the hole in the bracket and into the center of the anchor and tighten.*

5 *Check that the two brackets are level before tightening the screws. If your spirit level is too short, rest it on a piece of wood.*

6 *Set the window box into position across the bracket. Make sure it is securely in place.*

7 *Insert a window box liner to help preserve the outer box and provide an insulating layer for the plants.*

8 *Buy the plants. If you cannot plant them immediately, store in a cool place and keep well watered.*

9 *Add a layer of broken ceramic shards for drainage. Fill the box with potting soil, mixing in water-retaining granules and slow-release fertilizer granules following the instructions on the packet.*

10 *Insert the plants. Space the box plants evenly and fill in the gaps between them with geraniums and helichrysum. Plant the ground ivy at the front of the window box so that it trails over the edge.*

Brightening Bare Walls
WALL CONTAINERS

A LARGE EXPANSE of bare wall or fence can be turned into an attractive garden feature by adding a collection of wall pots planted with a variety of colorful plants. Use this opportunity to grow plants that are best admired at close quarters, such as those with arching flowers or intriguing markings. Bear in mind that wall pots usually don't contain a great deal of soil, so regular feeding and watering is essential.

Summer subtlety

Kingfisher daisy and wandering sailor are effectively contrasted here by golden feverfew. Convolvulus sabatius provides a trail of lilac flowers, helping to soften the hard lines of the sides of the pot. All the plants, apart from the feverfew, are frost tender, so wait until the end of the spring frosts before planting.

1 Kingfisher daisy (*Felicia bergeriana*)

2 Wandering sailor (*Tradescantia fluminensis*)

3 *Convolvulus sabatius*

4 Golden feverfew (*Tanacetum parthenium* 'Aureum')

PLANTING ALTERNATIVES

Spring shades

A collection of wall pots containing spring-flowering woodland plants makes a beautiful feature for the gloomy early months. Lenten roses come in limitless subtle shades and mixtures, but you may not know which color you have until they flower for the first time. Plant the Lenten roses in a liner so that you can lift them out of the pot once the flowers are over and replace them with new specimens for summer.

2 Purple Lenten rose (*Helleborus* x *hybridus*)

1 White Lenten rose (*Helleborus* x *hybridus*)

3 Ivy (*Hedera helix* 'Eva')

Orange cascade

For a warmer color scheme, substitute the plants listed below for those illustrated.

1 *Tropaeolum majus* 'Alaska'

3 Black-eyed Susan (*Thunbergia alata*)

4 Snapdragon (*Antirrhinum* 'Coronette') – salmon pink variety

PROJECT PLANNER

TIME SCALE **1** HOUR

Tools and Materials

Wall pot • Masonry drill and bit • Anchor • Screw and screwdriver • Broken ceramic shards • Potting soil • Slow-release fertilizer granules • Water-retaining granules

1 *Wall pots come in various shapes, sizes, and materials. Choose a style and color to complement the wall on which it is to be positioned.*

2 *Buy the plants. If you cannot plant them immediately, store them in a cool place and keep well watered.*

3 *Put up the wall pot. Drill a hole in the wall and tap in an anchor that is large enough to fit the hole snuggly.*

4 *Position the pot and screw. Tighten, making sure you leave enough of the screw projecting from the wall to support the pot.*

5 *Place broken ceramic shards in the bottom of the pot. Fill with potting soil, mixing in water-retaining and slow-release fertilizer granules following the manufacturer's instructions.*

6 *Plant the pot, following the instructions on page 30. Water thoroughly.*

MAINTENANCE

• *Remove dead flowers and straggly stems as they appear.*

• *Six weeks after planting, add liquid fertilizer to the water, following the manufacturer's instructions.*

• *In the fall, replace the plants with spring-flowering bulbs. Reuse the ivy if it is in good condition. Discard the kingfisher daisy and replant the feverfew elsewhere. Wandering sailor and convolvulus can be repotted and overwintered somewhere frost free. Both will make new plants from cuttings taken in late summer or early fall (see page 39).*

Water Feature for a Small Space
POND IN A BARREL

IN ANY GARDEN, a pond – even if it is only a small one – immediately becomes a focal point. Water has the effect of attracting birds and insect life to a garden, and a pond provides an instant "lift" for any characterless area.

If you don't have the right type of garden to set a pond into the ground, you can create a potted pond in any watertight container – in a large ceramic pot, for example, a stone sink (once the drain hole is tightly plugged), or, as here, a wooden half-barrel. Check that your barrel is suitable for turning into a pond – those designed for planting may have large gaps between the slats. A barrel that once held liquid will be waterproof once it has been thoroughly soaked. Always include an oxygenating species, such as *Elodea canadensis*, to help keep the water fresh. Around the pond you can stand pots of bog plants that look appropriate with a water feature, such as hostas, primulas, or ferns.

White water lilies

This wooden half-barrel was made into a miniature pond for a sunny corner of the garden. The white-flowered pygmy water lily and the pale-green water lettuce spread over the surface of the water, nestling around the upright dwarf cattail that creates contrast and adds height to the feature.

1 Dwarf cattail (*Typha minima*)

2 Water lettuce (*Pistia stratiotes*)

3 Pygmy water lily (*Nymphaea* 'Pygmaea Alba')

PLANTING ALTERNATIVES

Scarlet cardinal flowers

For a more vibrant color scheme, substitute the plants listed below for those shown in the illustration. Here, the upright form of the scarlet cardinal flower replaces the pygmy water lily. It is not very hardy, however, and so you may need to transfer it to a bucket and keep it in a frost-free place over winter. The dwarf cattail can remain, since it is small enough for a tiny pond such as this. Parrot's feather is exchanged for water lettuce to provide a more feathery-looking cover at water level.

2 Parrot's feather
(*Myriophyllum aquaticum*)

3 Cardinal flower
(*Lobelia cardinalis*)

Blue water irises

A spiky clump of deep, rich blue Japanese water iris replaces the cattail to provide that all-essential vertical feature of the planting. Parrot's feather spreads over the surface of the water, as in the scarlet-colored planting above, while fairy moss is substituted for the water lily.

1 Japanese water iris
(*Iris laevigata* 'Midnight')

2 Parrot's feather
(*Myriophyllum aquaticum*)

3 Fairy moss
(*Azolla mexicana*)

PROJECT PLANNER

TIME SCALE **1+** HOURS

Tools and Materials

Wooden barrel (suitable for holding water) • Stiff brush • Hose • Gravel • Brick

1 *Clean the barrel thoroughly with a stiff brush and fill with water. Keep refilling the barrel over a period of 24 hours. Wet wood expands, and this will ensure that the barrel is watertight.*

2 *Place the barrel where you intend to plant it. Place a brick in the center of the barrel. The major feature of the planting — a water lily — will stand on this. Buy the plants. Keep them in water in the shade until you are ready to put them in the barrel.*

3 *Stand the water plants in their containers in the barrel.*

4 *Spread a layer of washed gravel over the soil of each plant in its container. Place floating water plants on the water's surface.*

MAINTENANCE

• *Remove any floating weed colonizing the pond by fishing it out with a kitchen sieve.*

• *Remove blanket weed by inserting a garden stake into it. Twist the stake until the weed starts to entangle and then pull it out.*

• *Cut back any plant that is growing too vigorously. Aim to leave about a quarter of the water's surface uncovered.*

• *Add water as necessary.*

• *Clear out dead plant growth and loose soil in both the fall and spring to prevent the water from becoming acrid.*

• *In the fall, lift out the pot of frost-tender water lettuce and place it in a bucket of clean water. Store it in a frost-free place. Replant in the barrel in late spring or early summer, once all danger of frost has passed.*

LAWNS

Glorious grass
A pristine, weed-free lawn sets off beds, borders, and other garden features beautifully. This rounded lawn, framed by trellises and climbing plants, provides a calm oasis of greenery amidst the extravagant growth all around.

Ideas for Improving Lawns

EASY TO CREATE and straightforward to maintain, for many people the lawn is the centerpiece of their garden. An impressive sweep of lawn – or even a tiny square of grass – makes a perfect foil for surrounding flower beds and borders.

Remember that a lawn can be far more than an ornamental showpiece: it has many functional uses, too – a means of access from one part of the garden to another; a place to relax and sunbathe with family and friends; a play area for the children, to name a few. The type of grass-seed mixture that you choose depends on how you use your lawn: if one of its main uses is as a football field for the kids, for example, then you will need a hard-wearing type (see page 74).

The questions on these two pages are designed to help you pinpoint ways in which you can improve your existing lawn, or create a new one, in order to enhance your garden. Each one is backed up by a step-by-step project that, where appropriate, includes suggestions for plants to use in your own garden.

? *Is there an area of your lawn that gets worn through constant use?*

Lay a series of stepping stones across it to protect the grass. This will look attractive and maintenance will be easier and less time-consuming. *Right:* These stepping stones reduce wear and tear on the grass and invite you to explore the rest of the garden.
SEE *Protecting Worn Lawns, page 80.*

? *Is your lawn a harsh, geometric shape?*

Choosing plants that overhang the edges of the lawn is a good way to soften the shape and create an informal look.
SEE *Softening Lawn Edges, page 78.*

❓ *Are you making a new lawn from scratch?*

You can choose between laying turves (expensive but quick) or establishing a lawn from seed (much cheaper but slower).

Right: A well-kept lawn is a credit to your garden and is the perfect setting for your beds and borders.

SEE *Growing a Lawn from Seed, page 74; Laying a Lawn from Turf, page 76.*

❓ *Does your lawn slope at an angle?*

Putting in steps will make it easier for you to navigate it — particularly in wet weather, when the grass is slippery.

Above: Here, lengths of treated wood form shallow steps to create an unusual, rustic-looking pathway.

SEE *Sloping Lawns, page 82.*

Growing a Lawn from Seed
COST-EFFECTIVE SOWING

THE BEST and most beautiful lawns are a real labor of love, but you can grow a good-looking and hard-wearing lawn that you can be proud of with relatively little effort.

If your existing lawn has more bald patches than grass, or if you've inherited a site that has never been grassed over, you'll need to create a new lawn. Decide if you want to grow a lawn from seed or from ready-grown turf (see chart, opposite). If you are sowing from seed, the best time to sow is in the fall, while the soil is still warm, although spring sowing is also acceptable. Do not subject a seed-sown lawn to heavy traffic for at least a year after sowing. Although a lawn grown from seed takes longer to establish itself than a lawn

---

PROJECT PLANNER

TIME SCALE ½ DAY

Tools and Materials
Cultivator • Rake • Garden twine • Garden roller (optional) • Fertilizer • Lawn Seed • Hay
The time scale given above is for an area measuring about 10 ft x 10 ft (3 m x 3 m)

2 *Next, rake the surface of your soil to remove any existing stones and debris on the plot, and to break up any large lumps of soil.*

3 *Using a rake, push and pull the surface layer of soil. This will further break down any lumps in the soil and smooth out bumps and hollows in your plot.*

1 *Remove any large stones and deep-rooted weeds from the site. Rent a cultivator and cultivate the soil to a depth of about 2 in (5 cm).*

4 *Firm down the soil surface by treading it down with your heels.*

5 *Mark out the lawn area using rope or twine. Apply granular fertilizer that contains nitrogen, potassium, and phosphorous, and sprinkle the recommended amount evenly over the soil. Inset: Rake in the fertilizer.*

6 *Measure the amount of grass seed recommended on the packet and sprinkle evenly over the soil, working backward so you don't stand on newly sown areas.*

7 *Spread hay over the seeded area to keep off birds. It will mulch into the lawn. Once the grass is 2–3 in (5–7.5 cm) long, cut it using a rotary mower.*

grown from turf, it is considerably less expensive and a greater variety of seed mixtures is available.

Designing your lawn

The size and shape of your lawn affect the look of your garden. A long, narrow lawn tends to draw the eye down along it, creating a long, narrow appearance, whereas a broad expanse of lawn across the width of the garden makes it seem wider. Use these optical illusions to your advantage when planning the shape of a new lawn, or when altering the shape of an existing one. To make a short garden seem longer, make wide beds or features on each side of the lawn and maximize its short length by tapering it toward one corner. To minimize the length of your garden, divide it crossways to break up the length and create garden areas within the garden.

Wide lawns with narrow flower beds along the edges can be a mistake. If you prefer flower beds bordering a lawn, make sure that the beds are at least 1 yd (1 m) wide – even if it means that your lawn is reduced to a strip rather than an expanse. this makes your flower beds a positive feature in their own right, rather than

little decorations at the edge of your lawn. If your gardening time is too limited to maintain such large areas of planting, then forget about borders altogether and give the whole area over to lawn. Add island beds of specimen trees and shrubs gradually as you feel the need and have the time to look after them.

SEED VS TURF

New lawn from seed

PROS
- Less expensive than turf
- More choice of varieties
- Watering not always essential

CONS
- Soil preparation must be thoroughly done
- You cannot walk on your new lawn for several weeks after sowing

New lawn from turf

PROS
- Gives an instant result
- Soil preparation does not need to be as thorough as for sowing from seed

CONS
- Costly
- Limited choice and variety of turfs
- Watering is usually essential – so you must have access to a water supply and hose

MAINTENANCE

Unless you want to encourage wild flowers to grow, apply a lawn fertilizer and selective weed killer in spring. Use a watering can with a dribble bar attachment to apply liquid formulations in strips, taking care not to overlap the strips.

In spring, use a fan-shaped spring-tined rake to remove winter debris before you mow for the first time.

In fall, use a spring-tined rake to remove matted grass and fallen leaves.

- *Mow to around 1 in (2.5 cm) or a little higher in dry weather. Vary the mowing pattern to avoid grooves in the lawn.*

- *Cut the lawn edges after mowing using long-handled shears; for awkward grass edges, such as the edge of steps, use single-handed shears. Alternatively, use either a gas-powered or electric weed-whacker for both areas.*

- *Always wear strong, thick-soled shoes or boots when mowing. If you're using an electric mower or trimmer, drape the cable over your shoulder to keep it away from the mower blades. Wear goggles when mowing long grass – particularly if it is stony or likely to contain hidden debris.*

- *Top dress the lawn in fall. Mix equal parts of coarse sand, sieved soil, and peat. Spread half a bucket per square yard (meter) over the lawn surface and rake it in.*

- *In fall, spike the lawn with a garden fork to improve drainage. Push the fork in vertically to a depth of 4–6 in (10–15 cm), then pull it out vertically.*

Laying a Lawn from Turf

INSTANT COVERAGE

YOU CAN LAY a new lawn from turf at any time of year except during dry, very wet, or freezing weather. The advantage of using ready-grown turf, rather than seed, is that it gives you a new lawn almost instantly. You need to avoid walking on new turf for two to three weeks after laying, until it starts to grow – but then you can treat it exactly as you would an established lawn.

Always examine the turf before you buy or accept delivery. Feel the soil under the turf to make sure that it is moist, not dry and crumbly, and unroll a couple of turves and check that the grass is dense and weed free.

Keep newly laid turf damp – otherwise the turves will shrink away from each other leaving large cracks. Water thoroughly and frequently, until the joints between the turves grow together.

PROJECT PLANNER

TIME SCALE 1/2 DAY

Tools and Materials

Rake • Fertilizer • Plank • Knife • Half-moon edger • Rope or twine • Sprinkler
The time scale given above is for an area measuring about 10 ft x 10 ft (3 m x 3 m)

1 Stack the turf close to your working area. Keep it damp and shaded until you are ready to lay the lawn.

2 Clear the site of stones, deep-rooted weeds and other debris. Rake the surface smooth and level several times. If necessary, loosen the top surface with a scuffle hoe. Tread the soil thoroughly all over to compact the surface and eliminate bumps and hollows, then sprinkle on fertilizer (see Step 5 of Growing A Lawn from Seed, page 74) and rake again.

3 Working from a side path or plank, unroll and position each turf in the first row. Stagger the next row of turves – to do this, you may have to cut a turf.

4 Butt the turves up tightly to one another, then tamp them down.

5 Don't position small pieces of turf at the edge of the lawn. Instead, make a gap in the lawn and cut a piece of turf to fit it.

6 Again working from a plank or side path, firmly tamp down the entire turfed area using the flat back of your rake.

7 Mark out the edge of the lawn using a rope or twine as a guide, then use a half-moon edging tool to cut the turf where necessary.

8 Water the turf thoroughly using a lawn sprinkler. Take care not to allow it to dry out until growth is well established.

LAWN REPAIR

To Repair Bumps and Hollows

1 *First, cut a cross in the turf as shown and peel back the edges.*

2 *Using a trowel, add, remove, or redistribute the soil under the turf to even out the bump or hollow.*

3 *Replace the flaps of turf and tamp down using the back of a rake. This can be done at any time between spring and fall.*

To Repair Ragged Edges

1 *Remove a rectangle of turf around the damaged edge and turn it around so that the damaged section is no longer on the edge.*

2 *Tamp down the turf and fill the hole with soil and a little grass seed. This can be done at any time between spring and fall.*

To Reseed Bare Patches

1 *Rake the soil to remove dead grass, pull up any weeds, and loosen the surface of the bare patch with a hand fork to create an area of fine soil.*

2 *Carefully scatter the grass seeds over the bare patch.*

3 *Speed up germination and protect the patch from birds by covering the area with a sheet of pierced clear plastic, pegged down to create a mini greenhouse. (If cats, rabbits, or other animals are a problem, use pegged-down chicken wire to protect the patch.) Remove the plastic covering once the grass seedlings are about 1 in (2.5 cm) high. Water in dry weather.*

Softening Lawn Edges
FRONT-LINE PLANTS

A LONG, STRAIGHT-EDGED lawn can look formal and severe in a garden setting. Use plants to break up the hard lines, make a softer and less regular shape, and give your garden a more informal and natural look.

It is important to choose plants that don't actually spread into or lie on the grass, since they would kill the turf. Instead, choose edging plants that arch over the edge of the lawn without getting tangled in the mower. Hardy geraniums (such as *Geranium macrorrhizum*) are an especially useful group of plants for the front of a grass-edged border; they make a low, neat hummock that can easily be nudged out of the way when mowing. Lady's mantle (*Alchemilla mollis*) and London pride (*Saxifraga* x *urbium*) are also pretty edging plants. To help to give a sense of unity to the whole garden, it is a good idea to make a repeating pattern of plants at the front of the bed or border.

The key to this critical "front line" between the grass and your garden plants lies in regular maintenance. Trim back the grass at the edge of the lawn every time you mow with single-handed shears to prevent it from invading the bed. While you're at it, you can trim any over-enthusiastic border plants.

Edging in lime yellow, silver, and purple

At the front edge of this border, four plants are used in a loosely repeating pattern that helps to give the planting unity. The purple-leaved heuchera and the silver-leaved lamb's ears contrast with the medium-green leaves and lime-green flowers of the lady's mantle and the glossy green of the elephant's ears. The fifth plant, Liriope muscari, *is set back slightly from the front of the border. It forms a tuft of spiky leaves and provides a visual break from the flatter, more horizontal forms of the plants in the front of the border.*

1 *Heuchera micrantha* 'Palace Purple'

2 *Liriope muscari*

3 Elephant's ears (*Bergenia cordifolia*)

MAINTENANCE

• *Water thoroughly in dry weather, especially during the first summer after planting.*

• *Clip back straggly growths that stray onto the lawn.*

• *Clip the lawn edges regularly – ideally every time you mow (see page 75).*

• *Cut back any old flowering stems once they are past their best.*

• *In fall or after flowering in spring, lift and divide overgrown clumps of elephant's ears (see page 39). Cut through the fleshy, horizontal underground stems (rhizomes) and replant the pieces.*

• *Replenish the bark-chip mulch in late spring, once the soil warms up.*

PROJECT PLANNER

TIME SCALE 1/2 DAY

Tools and Materials

Fork • Compost or manure • Rake • Trowel • Bark-chip mulch
The time scale above is for a site about 10 yd (10 m) long.

1 *Fork over the front 1 ft (30 cm) of the border soil, and enrich it by adding a bucketful of compost or manure every yard (meter). Tread down the soil and rake it smooth.*

2 *Buy the plants. If you are not able to plant them immediately, keep them watered and in the shade.*

3 *Plant the plants in groups of three or five, about 4–6 in (10–15 cm) from the front of the bed. Repeat the same planting pattern along the length of the bed.*

4 *Water thoroughly. Apply a 2–3-in (5–7.5-cm) layer of bark chippings as a mulch.*

4 Lamb's ears (*Stachys byzantina* 'Silver Carpet')

5 Lady's mantle (*Alchemilla mollis*)

PLANTING ALTERNATIVES

Edging in gold and white

To create a fresher, lighter effect, change the purple-leaved heuchera for green-leaved and white-flowered foam flower and the lamb's ears for white deadnettle. The *Liriope muscari*, elephant's ears, and lady's mantle remain, since they contrast well with the dark green leaves of the foam flower and the white-splashed leaves of the deadnettle.

1 Foam flower *(Tiarella cordifolia)*

4 White deadnettle *(Lamium maculatum 'Album')*

Protecting Worn Lawns
STEPPING-STONE PATH

ALMOST EVERY LAWN has areas that get more wear and tear than others. To protect the lawn, you can put in a stepping-stone path. This will also save you from having to reseed patches of lawn each year. Make a feature of the path by arranging the paving slabs in a pattern; children will enjoy making a game of hopping along the path.

The easiest method is to cut holes in the turf where each step will be, lift the turf, and replace it with a paving slab. The surrounding turf will hold the slab in place, so there is no need to use cement. You can use irregularly-shaped pieces of flat stone or regular-shaped manufactured slabs. Choose slabs that are big enough to stand on comfortably.

Short cut

Your path should always take the shortest route to encourage people to use it. Here, 18-in (45-cm) square paving slabs have been arranged in a formal style. The slabs are set just below the level of the lawn so that a mower can run over the slabs without damaging its blades or the path.

Diamond setting

Square paving slabs were set diagonally in staggered rows to create a repeating diamond pattern. This arrangement lends itself to creating a second path that branches off the first, if you should need it.

Meadow path

Pressure-treated log slices are ideal for a more natural-looking path, such as in a flowering meadow or an informally-planted shrubbery. Make sure the log slices have been treated with wood preservative to prevent them from rotting. If the route the path is to take is shaded, wrap each slice in chicken wire to create a slip-proof surface before laying them in your lawn.

PROJECT PLANNER

TIME SCALE 1/2 DAY

Tools and Materials

Paving slabs • Garden twine
• Half-moon cutter • Spade
• Coarse sand • Spirit level
• Hard bristle broom

1 *Lay the paving slabs across the lawn. To mark out a straight path, put down a taut line of garden twine and align the slabs with it. Make sure they are evenly spaced. Leave about 6 in (15 cm) of turf between each slab.*

2 *Cut around each slab using a half-moon cutter, cutting deep into the turf.*

3 *Using a spade, carefully lift out the section of turf you have cut.*

4 *Line the space with at least 2 in (5 cm) of coarse sand so that the slab lies just below the level of the rest of the turf.*

5 *Place the slab onto the sand. Check that it is set below the surface of the lawn and that it is level. Finally, sweep the slab clean.*

Sloping Lawns
INFORMAL STEPS

GENTLY SLOPING lawn can make a very attractive feature: it conjures up images of rolling countryside and, even if your garden is a small urban one, the smooth sweep of grass creates a tranquil, country feel.

From a practical point of view, however, a sloping lawn can be difficult to negotiate. In damp weather, when the lawn is likely to become slippery, it can be treacherous under foot. The solution is to inset gentle steps that can become an attractive feature of the lawn in their own right.

Rather than installing permanent steps, opt for the more natural look of informal bark steps shaped to fit your particular slope. They need not be parallel or even evenly spaced. The informality of this kind of step adds to the rural feel. Reseed any disturbed grass areas with a meadow-grass seed mixture to encourage some wild flowers to establish themselves.

Soft landings

Make a safe route across a sloping lawn. Here, wooden risers holding 3 in (7.5 cm) of chipped bark create a set of informal country-style steps.

ALTERNATIVE STEPS

Stone risers

For something a little more solid looking, use stone slabs 2–3 in (5–7.5 cm) deep and at least 10 in (25 cm) in length set on their edge as the risers. Make sure the stones are set at least 6 in (15 cm) deep, leaving 4 in (10 cm) exposed; their weight will keep them stable with no need for concrete. You can plant low ground-cover plants or meadow flowers along the edge of the steps.

MAINTENANCE

• *The edges of the steps, where you removed the turf, may be prone to weeds at first. Until the grass has grown back, check for weeds regularly and remove them as they appear.*

• *Use a weed-whacker after mowing to keep edges of the steps tidy.*

• *Replenish the bark chippings as necessary.*

PROJECT PLANNER

TIME SCALE **1/2 DAY**

Tools and Materials

Lengths of 4 x 1^{1}/$_{2}$ in (10 x 3.8 cm) pressure-treated soft wood • Pressure-treated stakes (2 per step) • Chisel • Spade • Metal piping • Mallet • 3-in (7.5-cm) galvanized nails • Hammer • Spirit level • Weed-barrier plastic • Large bark chippings
The time scale given above is for approx. 6 bark steps.

1 *Cut riser slats to the required length from 4 x 1.5 in (10 x 3.8 cm) pressure-treated soft wood and lay them across the slope wherever a step is needed. Make the steps descend gradually; each subsequent tread should be no more than 4 in (10 cm) below the previous one.*

2 *Make or buy pressure-treated pointed stakes to hold the risers in position. Bevel one end using a chisel.*

3 *Starting at the bottom of the slope and working uphill so that you can see the slope ahead of you, dig out the first tread to a depth of no more than 4 in (10 cm). Use a spirit level to check that it is level in all directions.*

4 *Make holes for the stakes by driving in a length of metal piping, marked to the required depth, with a mallet.*

5 *Nail a stake to each end of each riser. Position the stakes in the holes and place a spare piece of wood on top of each riser. Using a mallet, knock in each end of the riser until it is level across the slope.*

6 *Continue in the same way until you have dug out all the treads and positioned the risers. Line each tread with weed-barrier plastic and fill it with large bark chippings.*

PATHS AND PAVING

Stony ground
*The soft, muted colors of this brick paving
make a light, neutral background for the
profusion of colorful plants. The formality of
the paving design – alternate steps are laid out
in a pinwheel pattern – is softened by the
plants that overhang the edges.*

Ideas for Improving Paths and Paving

PATIOS AND PAVED areas have an important part to play in your enjoyment of your garden. They're great for entertaining – particularly if the weather has been wet or the dew heavy and you can't walk on the lawn without getting your feet wet. They also provide a wonderful setting for plants – but you need to choose your plants carefully. Paved and concreted surfaces are visually strong, and you need to counteract this by using strong-charactered plants around them – ones with large leaves and dramatic shapes and colors. In fact, paved areas need plants to soften their harsh lines.

Paths have obvious practical uses in enabling you to walk from one part of the garden to another. They can also provide a framework for your planting, dividing the garden into discrete sections. From an aesthetic point of view, they can be used to lead the eye to other features such as a garden ornament or arbor.

The questions on these two pages are designed to help you pinpoint ways in which you can improve your existing paths and paving, or create new ones, in order to enhance your garden. Each one is backed up by a step-by-step project that, where appropriate, includes suggestions for plants to use in your own garden.

? Do you have a path that is broken or unattractive?

An easy way to create a new path that is easy to maintain is to dig out most of an existing path and fill the area with gravel or cover it with wooden decking.

Right: This path is made of limestone chippings edged with railroad ties. Orange rock rose, green-flowered hellebores, and pink potentilla soften the path edges.

SEE *Non-slip Path, page 94; Quick-and-easy Path, page 96.*

? Do you have gaps between paving?

Make a virtue of them by planting in the cracks.

Left: The texture of these slabs contrasts with the lady's mantle and the pebbles between the widely spaced paving.

SEE *Planting between Paving Slabs, page 92.*

? Do your paved areas have straight edges?

You can soften the overall shape, and introduce an informal effect, by planting overhanging plants around the edges of your paving.

Left: An attractive cloud of lady's mantle sprawls over the hard edges of this paved path.

SEE *Softening Paving Edges, page 88.*

? Do you have a large area of dull paving?

You can brighten up a paved area by removing occasional slabs and planting in the spaces you create.

SEE *Livening up Paving, page 90.*

Softening Paving Edges
BREAKING THE LINE

PATIO AREAS ARE often geometric in shape. Although many people welcome such neat, tidy shapes, they can look bare and stark – not the sort of place you would want to sit and relax in for any length of time.

To soften a paved patio's appearance, allow plants to billow over the edges of the paving to create a gentler overall effect. The best plants to use are ones that have strong enough shapes and shadows to counteract the hardness and flatness of the paving material. Dramatic shapes are better than indistinct ones: fine, feathery foliage such as that of cotton lavender is not as effective as large bold leaves characteristic of hosta.

Patios are often next to the house and in full view, so make sure you have a planting that will provide an attractive show throughout the year. The planting scheme illustrated below uses evergreens to provide a basic framework. You can introduce seasonal changes by adding winter- and spring-flowering bulbs and some summer bedding plants.

Evergreens in blue, purple, and gray

Although the dramatic clump of purple phormium does not actually overlap the edge of the paving, its bold outline casts leafy shadows that draw attention away from the hard, flat surface. A variegated, white-flowered deadnettle carpets the spaces between the other plants. The spreading blue-gray juniper makes an excellent contrast to the phormium in both its habit and color. Jerusalem sage is a handsome gray-leaved evergreen that provides a splash of yellow flowers in summer.

1 Jerusalem sage
(Phlomis fruticosa)

2 Deadnettle (*Lamium maculatum* 'White Nancy')

MAINTENANCE

- *Snip off any untidy or dead growth.*
- *Remove dead flower heads of Jerusalem sage.*
- *Water regularly in dry weather — especially in the first summer before the plants are well established.*

4 Phormium tenax

PROJECT PLANNER

TIME SCALE **1/2 DAY**

Tools and Materials

Fork • Manure or garden compost • Rake • Trowel • Bark-chip mulch
The time scale above is for a site about 10 yd (10 m) long.

1 *Fork over the front 2 ft (60 cm) of soil bordering the paving. Enrich by adding a bucketful of manure or garden compost every yard (meter). Tread down the soil and rake it smooth.*

2 *Buy the plants. If you can't plant them immediately, keep them in the shade and water daily.*

3 *Plant the Jerusalem sage, juniper, and phormium at least 1 ft (30 cm) from the front edge of the bed, staggering their positions slightly so that they are not in a straight line. Plant the deadnettle in front of the phormium and in any big gaps along the front edge.*

4 *Water thoroughly and apply a 2-in (5-cm) layer of bark-chip mulch over the soil between the plants.*

PLANTING ALTERNATIVES

Golden foliage

For a warmer color scheme, swap the blue-gray creeping juniper for a golden variety. Change the ground-covering deadnettle for yellow-flowered archangel and the phormium for a smaller, but still imposing, daylily with yellow flowers. The yellow flowers of Jerusalem sage work equally well with this golden color scheme, so it can remain as a source of summer color.

2 Yellow archangel (*Lamium galeobdolon* 'Variegatum')

3 Ground-cover variegated juniper (*Juniperus* x *media* 'Carbery Gold')

4 Daylily (*Hemerocallis* 'Marion Vaughn')

3 Creeping juniper (*Juniperus squamata* 'Blue Carpet')

Livening up Paving
AROMATIC PATIO CORNER

LIVEN UP YOUR paving and create a conversation-stopping showpiece by replacing occasional stone slabs with unique plantings. Make a repeating pattern of planting spaces to emphasize the corners or edges of your patio or to create a division in the paving – marking off an eating area from a sitting area, for example.

Choose plants that tolerate shallow soil, as they require little watering and are thus easier to care for. Many herbs, desert, and rock plants fall into this category. The planting suggestion below, which uses a range of low-growing herbs, is a particularly good choice for a paved area near the house, as the herbs are easily accessible for cooking.

Contrast the texture of the plants with the texture of the paving, alternating squares of soft, cushion-like plants, such as the herbs shown below, with hard, flat, concrete slabs, for example. Color is important, too: the gold-green and purple plants below work well with the natural beige of the paving slabs.

Herbal checkerboard

Herbs are a great choice for planting in paving since many of them like poor, well-drained soil. They have the added benefit of a delicious aroma, which you can enjoy as you pass by. Here, edged with purple bugle, a small collection of thymes and golden marjoram is arranged in a checkerboard pattern.

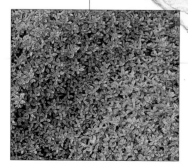

1 Golden thyme (*Thymus* x *citriodorus* 'Aureus')

90

PLANTING ALTERNATIVES

Rock-plant checkerboard

For an alternative planting scheme, use rock and alpine plants in place of the herbs. Replace the two thymes with thrift (*Armeria maritima*) and the marjoram with alpine aster. This is a simpler design that emphasizes the contrasting forms of the thrift and the aster. For edging, replace the bugle with New Zealand burr: its burnished coloring sets off the dark pink thrift and the purple aster. Cover the soil between the plants with a mulch of gravel after planting.

1 and **3** Thrift (*Armeria maritima*)

2 New Zealand burr (*Acaena microphylla*)

4 Alpine aster (*Aster alpinus*)

4 Golden marjoram (*Origanum vulgare* 'Aureum')

3 Thyme (*Thymus vulgaris* 'Silver Posie')

2 Purple variegated bugle (*Ajuga reptans* 'Atropurpurea')

PROJECT PLANNER

TIME SCALE ½ DAY

Tools and Materials

Mallet • Chisel • Spade • Topsoil • Trowel

The time scale above is for a site about 4 sq yd (4 sq m).

1 *Pry up the paving slabs that you want to remove. If they are bedded in concrete, you will need to break up the mortar joints with a mallet and chisel first. Inset: If the slabs are set in sand, use a spade to lift them up.*

2 *Break up any mortar under the slabs with the mallet and chisel, and remove it.*

3 *Cover the planting space with topsoil and plant (see page 32). Water thoroughly.*

MAINTENANCE

• *Keep watered and weeded. You may need to weed out over-vigorous bugle stems to prevent them from overwhelming the other plants.*

• *Trim the thymes and marjoram in summer to keep them in shape. You can use the clippings in cooking.*

Planting between Paving Slabs
SELF-SEEDING FLOWERS

PLANTING SELF-SEEDING flowers between paving slabs is a very simple, but eye-catching way of brightening up your paving. Choose plants that enjoy the sparse, often alkaline, soil of paved areas. They will seed themselves, leaving you with little to do beyond occasionally thinning them out if they grow too profusely. Suitable plants include many of the alpines, herbs, annual flowers, and short-lived perennials.

This is a particularly useful idea if your paving is old and cracked: instead of going to the expense and disruption of laying new surfaces, make a virtue out of something that many people might consider a defect. Weathered paving has a character and charm that you simply do not find in pristine, newly laid paving and looks particularly good with old-fashioned "cottage garden" and wild flowers.

Shaded paving

*This attractive planting is ideal for a shaded patio or paved area. The Welsh poppy (*Meconopsis cambrica*) and heartsease (*Viola tricolor*) flower from the late spring through the summer months and the Corsican mint (*Mentha requienii*) provides color throughout most of the year. The bright yellow poppy combines well with the delicate violet and the rich green foliage of the mint to create a striking display reminiscent of a traditional cottage garden. The mint exudes a wonderful scent when crushed underfoot and its sprawling leaves will reach across the paving, creating interesting shapes within your site.*

1 Heartsease
(*Viola tricolor*)

PLANTING ALTERNATIVES

Sunny paving

For a paved area that receives a lot of sunlight, substitute the plants below for those illustrated. Exchange the shade-loving Corsican mint and the Welsh poppy for a sun-worshipping creeping thyme such as *Thymus serpyllum* 'Goldstream' and the field poppy (*Papaver rhoeas*). Leave the heartsease, as it is happy in either sun or shade and will help to create a colorful show.

2 Creeping thyme (*Thymus serpyllum* 'Goldstream')

3 Field poppy (*Papaver rhoeas*)

2 Welsh poppy
(*Meconopsis cambrica*)

3 Corsican mint
(*Mentha requienii*)

PROJECT PLANNER

TIME SCALE 1+ HOURS

Tools and Materials

Chisel • Mallet • Narrow trowel • Soil-based compost • Fine soil • Chicken wire • Wire pegs or skewers

1 *Clean out the gaps in the paving with the chisel and mallet and remove any loose material with the trowel.*

2 *Fill the cracks with soil-based compost.*

3 *Sow seed thinly in the cracks and cover with fine soil. Inset: Cover with chicken wire held in place with wire pegs or skewers until the seedlings are well established to prevent the seeds from being eaten by birds.*

4 *Water the seedlings in dry weather. Thin out the seedlings when they become overcrowded. Replant the excess seedlings elsewhere to help integrate the paved area with the rest of the garden.*

MAINTENANCE

• *Cut the poppies down to ground level once the seedheads are dry.*

• *Shake the contents of the seedheads over the ground to encourage self-seeding.*

• *Deadhead the heartsease (unless you want it to self-sow).*

• *Snip off any straggly mint stems.*

• *Encourage the mint stems to root by pushing them into the paving cracks.*

Non-slip Path
FORMAL GRAVEL FEATURE

AN ELEGANT GRAVEL PATH is perfect for a garden that is formal in style – and it is one of the easiest paths to make. It is also practical: because water drains through the gravel, you can walk on it after rain without worrying about it being slippery.

Some kind of edging needs to be placed along the sides of the path in order to contain the gravel. For this reason, most gravel paths are straight – it is the straight lines that give such paths their formal appearance.

Sketch your design first to make sure that you get the proportions right. Make decorative paths wide enough to stroll along comfortably and balance them with beds of at least the same width. Experiment with different arrangements – paths radiating out in four directions from a central octagonal bed, perhaps, or a single path edging a rectangular lawn.

Gravel and stone chippings come in various sizes and colors, from slate gray to golden brown. The smallest $^1/_2$-in (1.25-cm) size will be difficult to walk on if it is more than 1 in (2.5. cm) deep. If your path has to be more than 1 in (2.5 cm) deep, lay a bed of $^3/_4$-in (2-cm) gravel underneath the small chippings.

Golden gravel walk

Intersecting gravel paths form a diagonal cross between triangular flower beds. Trees were positioned to create intriguing views through their branches and bring some height and a little shade to the area. Plants were allowed to overlap the path edging and soften its straight lines.

MAINTENANCE

• *Keep the path weeded: remove any weeds as soon as they emerge. Try not to get any soil on the gravel, since weeds will quickly grow in it.*

• *Add new gravel when necessary and rake smooth.*

PROJECT PLANNER

TIME SCALE 1 DAY

Tools and Materials

Garden twine • Tape measure • Spade • Rake • Pointed pressure-treated lumber pegs, 2 x 2 x 18 in (5 x 5 x 45 cm) • Mallet • Pressure-treated 5 x 1 in (12.5 x 2.5 cm) boards • 3-in (7.5-cm) galvanized nails • Weed-barrier plastic • Gravel

The time scale given above is for a path 10 yd (10 m) long.

1 *Mark out the path, using garden twine and a tape measure and rake the ground and tread it firm and level. Dig a 2-in (5-cm) deep slit at each side of the path and carefully insert the gravel boards. Make sure that the edges are straight and parallel. Tap the boards down with a mallet to secure.*

2 *Using a mallet, knock pointed pegs into the ground on the outside edge of the path wherever two boards meet. (This reinforces the join.) The pegs should be level with or just below the boards. Nail the pegs to the boards using 3-in (7.5-cm) galvanized nails.*

3 *Lay weed-barrier plastic along the floor of the path. Trim it to fit the path if necessary.*

4 *Pour in the gravel and spread it evenly over the path. It should be 1–2 in (2.5–5 cm) deep all along the path.*

5 *Rake the gravel smooth. The final level should be about 1 in (2.5 cm) below the top of the gravel board.*

Quick-and-easy Path
DECKING WALKWAY

IF YOU'VE ALWAYS DESIRED a stylish, refined-looking wooden walkway but feared that it would be too difficult or time-consuming to construct yourself, hesitate no more: wooden decking tiles are the answer. Packs of ready-made, pretreated tiles are inexpensive and available at many home and garden stores. Your only requirement is that the ground must be flat: if it is bumpy or sloping, you will need a lumber substructure to hold the walkway securely above ground — in which case you may want to hire a contractor to help.

Decking tiles make particulary good paths through flower beds if you need a short cut to another area of the garden. They're also useful as temporary paths to lay across an area that's occasionally muddy.

You can even color your decking, as woodstains are available in a number of different colors — but make sure you buy one that is suitable for exterior use. The stain should be renewed every few years.

Decking path through shrubbery
Decking tiles, staggered to create a more interesting shape, are used to create a convenient pathway through a bed of shrubs. Bark chippings scattered alongside the path ensure that the contrast between the decking and the adjoining bed is not too stark.

96

PROJECT PLANNER

TIME SCALE 2 HOURS

Tools and Materials

Garden twine • Rake • Spirit level • Decking tiles • Weed-barrier plastic • Wire pegs • Mallet • Pointed pressure-treated lumber pegs, 2 x 2 x 18 in (5 x 5 x 45 cm) • Large bark chippings
The time scale given above is for a path 10 yd (10 m) long

1 *Before you begin, plan the route of the path and mark out its outer edges with garden twine. Rake the path smooth and use a spirit level to check that it is completely level.*

2 *Set the tiles in position, butting them up to one another to check that they are arranged the way that you want them.*

3 *Remove the tiles and lay weed-barrier plastic along the route of the path, pinning it down with wire pegs.*

4 *Lay the tiles in position on top of the weed-barrier plastic, butting them up to each other.*

5 *Using a mallet, knock a treated wooden peg in through the weed-barrier plastic at each corner of each tile to secure in place.*

6 *Cover the exposed weed-barrier plastic with large bark chippings.*

Forming patterns

Experiment with laying the tiles at different angles to form patterns. Here, the tiles are placed at right angles to each other, forming a pattern similar to a basket weave.

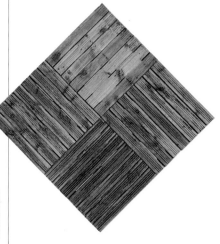

MAINTENANCE

• *Keep the path clear of mud, leaves, and algae since these will make it slippery.*

• *Remove any weeds that emerge through the slats.*

• *Wash the decking with a hose and a stiff broom if it gets muddy.*

• *If you use a colored stain on the tiles, renew it every few years.*

• *Check the tiles once a year for splits or cracks and replace any that are badly damaged.*

WALLS, FENCES, AND HEDGES

Beautiful boundaries
Beautiful flowering climbers, such as the magnificent white rose, Rosa filipes *'Kiftsgate', make this wall an attractive garden feature. This vibrant splash of color provides a striking contrast to the plain brickwork of the wall and makes an inviting entrance to the area beyond the gate.*

Ideas for Improving Walls, Fences, and Hedges

THE EXTERNAL boundaries of your garden – the walls, fences, and hedges – provide the basic framework against which all of your plantings are seen. They also have a practical effect on the micro-climate of your garden, creating shelter and shade and therefore influencing the type of plants that you can grow. When you choose plants, you need to think not only about factors such as shade, but also about aesthetic considerations – how your plants will blend in or contrast with the boundaries in terms of their color and texture.

Something that many people overlook is that walls, fences, and hedges can also be used as internal divisions – separating a patio area from the rest of the garden, or creating a secluded corner where you can enjoy the afternoon sunshine.

The questions on these two pages are designed to help you pinpoint ways in which you can improve existing boundaries, or create new ones, in order to enhance your garden. Each one is backed up by a step-by-step project that includes suggestions for plants that you might like to use in your own garden.

? Does your garden feel too open?

Set up boundaries within the garden to create a separate "garden room" or a series or "rooms" and make it more interesting to walk through. *Right:* This garden sanctuary is created by 7-ft (2.1 m) high yew hedging. The petunias and potted marguerite daisies match the striking white statue. SEE *A Garden Divider, page 110; Formal Hedge, page 114.*

? Does your front-yard fence look dilapidated?

With a minimum of practical skills, you can create an informal fence that also makes the perfect frame for plants to grow on and around. SEE *Front-Yard Boundary, page 118.*

? *Do buildings enclose or overlook your garden?*

Raise the height of boundary walls and fences (be sure to check any local ordinances) and grow climbers up them to make them look more attractive. *Above*: A trellis, covered in the beautiful *Rosa* 'Handel', increases the height of the low wall and prevents the garden from being overlooked.
SEE *Heightening a Wall with Trellis, page 104*

? *Is your hedge an expanse of single color?*

Plant a flowering hedge or train a succession of flowering climbers through an evergreen hedge to give seasonal variety and color. *Above*: The colorful splendor of this beautiful garden overflows into the hedges. The clipped, dark-green yew cone is enhanced by the flame-colored nasturtium.
SEE *Adding Color to Green Hedges, page 108;
Informal Boundary Hedge, page 112.*

? *Do your bed and border edges look untidy?*

Plant a miniature hedge to define the edges.
Left: This miniature box hedge makes a neat edging to the bed and hides the bare rose stems. Alpine daisies and catmint cascade over the wall in front of the hedge.
SEE *Defining Your Beds, page 116.*

? *Do you have a fence or boundary that is bare and boring?*

Use trellis panels to break up a blank wall area and train climbers and wall shrubs through the trellis to soften the edges. If the wall gets the sun, you can create a scented sitting area.
SEE *Enhancing a Bare Wall, page 102;
Plants for a Sunny Wall, page 106.*

Enhancing a Bare Wall
LIVING TRELLIS

MANY GARDENS, especially in towns and cities where space is scarce and houses are packed tightly together, are hemmed in by a tall, blank wall. For a conversation-stopping show piece, put up a trellis and train plants over it. This project features horizontally-trained firethorns that have been pruned to leave a main vertical stem with several horizontal side stems emerging on either side.

Living wall for a shaded site
Here the firethorn plants have been pruned tightly back to cover their stems with foliage and create a living trellis effect. Their scarlet berries are accentuated in the fall by the bright red leaves of Virginia creeper. Evergreen euonymous smothers the ground.

One of the problems with this type of situation is that tall walls often shade the soil beneath them from rain and light. The design below uses firethorn and Virginia creeper, both of which thrive in dry, impoverished soil and shade. If you have a sunny wall, try training a fruit tree (an apple, plum, pear, or cherry) in the same way.

1 Virginia creeper (*Parthenocissus quinquefolia*)

2 Firethorn (*Pyracantha* 'Mohave')

MAINTENANCE

• *Keep the site well weeded and watered and mulch in late spring or fall.*

• *Prune unwanted growth in summer.*

• *Tie horizontal stems of the firethorn to the trellis as they grow, using plastic-covered wire twists or garden twine. Check the ties occasionally, loosening them if necessary to allow the stems room to grow.*

• *Prune the firethorn in the summer months. Pinch out any shoots that are growing in the wrong place as they emerge. Leave shoots that are growing in the right direction to grow to the required length. Allow these stems to grow side shoots 2–4 in (5–10 cm) in length to clothe the main stem.*

3 Pink-tinged *Euonymus* such as 'Variegata'

PROJECT PLANNER

TIME SCALE 1/2 DAY

Tools and Materials

Trellis panel • Spirit level • Pencil or chalk • Treated 2 x 1-in (5 x 2.5-cm) wooden battens • Screws and screwdriver • Drill with wood and masonry drill bits • Nails • Anchors • Spade • Compost or manure • Bone meal • Fork • Rake • Tree stake • Wire ties • Pruning shears

1 *Position the trellis panel on the wall. Using a spirit level, check that it is straight. Mark its position on the wall with a pencil or chalk.*

2 *Postion the battens vertically on the wall in line with the markings. At 18-in (45-cm) intervals, make screw holes in the battens.*

3 *Tap a nail through each batten screw hole into the wall to mark the screw positions. Then drill holes in the wall at each screw point using a masonry drill bit.*

4 *Insert anchors into the wall screw holes and screw the battens to the wall. Screw the trellis panel to the battens, using a spirit level to check that it is straight and level.*

5 *Prepare the ground at the base of the wall, forking in plenty of compost or manure. Plant the firethorn, (see page 33), using a tree stake to support the main vertical stem so that it grows straight. You can remove the stake once the plant has reached the required height.*

6 *Spread out the horizontal branches of the firethorn. Remove any that are wrongly placed, cutting them back flush with the main stem. Tie those that are growing in the right direction to the trellis, using wire ties.*

7 *Plant a Virginia creeper at either end of the trellis to soften the edges and to create a frame for the planting. Plant the euonymus in front of the trellis.*

Heightening a Wall with Trellis
PLANTS FOR PRIVACY

THERE ARE SEVERAL reasons why you might want to raise the height of a wall or fence – to hide an unnatractive view, to grow a particular climbing plant and show it off to its full glory, or simply to improve your privacy.

The best way to do this is to purchase a rigid trellis from a garden center – they come with slats of differing widths to choose from. You can make your own – but be sure to use pressure-treated lumber that is suitable for garden use. Alternatively, you can use a folding lightweight diamond-pattern trellis. However, this type is flimsy, and thus recommended only as a temporary measure. It is sometimes recommended for garden security, since it will not bear the weight of someone climbing over it.

The design below raises a 4-ft (1.3-m) wall by placing an 18-in (45-cm) rigid trellis, covered with climbing plants, on top. The trellis lets through some light and air and is more neighbor-friendly than a solid fence or wall. The total height of the fence should be roughly at eye level: a wall or fence that is lower than this invites people to look over it. A fence higher than eye level cuts down the amount of light entering your garden.

A sunny screen of climbers

Here, some attractive, shaped trellis panels were added to a 4-ft (1.3-m) garden wall to create an opportunity to grow climbers and to provide privacy in the summer months. The climbers chosen provide a good spread of interest throughout the spring and summer months.

1 Honeysuckle (*Lonicera periclymenum* 'Serotina')

2 Passionflower (*Passiflora* 'Amethyst')

104

3 Crimson glory vine (*Vitis coignetiae*)

PROJECT PLANNER

TIME SCALE **1/2 DAY**

Tools and Materials

Spirit level ● Chalk or pencil ● 3 x 3-in (7.5 x 7.5-cm) fence posts ● Drill with masonry and standard bits ● Tape measure ● Anchors ● 4-in (10-cm) screws ● Screwdriver ● Trellis panels ● Trellis brackets (6 for each trellis panel) ● Post caps ● Hammer ● Manure or compost ● Fork ● Rake ● Trowel ● Bone meal
The time scale given above is for putting up 3–4 trellis panels.

1 *Using a spirit level and chalk or a pencil, mark the position of the fence posts on the wall. Put the posts against the wall. Use a masonry drill bit, drill holes about 18-in (45-cm) apart through the posts and into the brickwork. Hammer anchors through the posts and into the wall.*

2 *Insert 4-in (10-cm) screws into the anchors in the wall and tighten.*

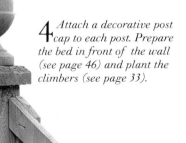

4 *Attach a decorative post cap to each post. Prepare the bed in front of the wall (see page 46) and plant the climbers (see page 33).*

3 *Hold the trellis panel in position and carefully mark where it should be attached to the posts. Put the panel down. Drill pilot holes and screw the brackets to the posts. Inset: Place the trellis panels in position and screw them to the brackets.*

MAINTENANCE

● *In late spring or fall, mulch with compost after watering.*

● *Entwine the stems of the climbers through the trellis as they grow.*

● *Prune the climbers, as necessary, in spring or fall (see page 43).*

● *Remove any dead, spindly growth in spring.*

● *Once a year, make sure that the posts and the trellis are still secure.*

● *Keep the plants weeded and watered.*

Plants for a Sunny Wall

SCENTED SEATING AREA

Asunny wall or fence swathed in climbing plants is a joy to behold. A comfortable bench can transform it into a pleasant sitting area in which you can relax. By planting on each side of the bench you can help to make the area feel enclosed and secret – your own special place.

The best plants for a seating area – especially on a still summer's evening when their perfume lingers in the air – are scented species. Lavender and other herbs that release a heady scent are always popular choices.

If you are planting behind a garden bench or seat, choose subjects that are tall enough to be seen and that don't mind their bases being in shade. Flowering tobacco is used in the planting below. Lilies are another good choice – the many species and varieties available give you a range of heights, from the 3–4 ft (1–1.2 m) regal lily to the 6–7 ft (2–2.1 m) *Lilium henryi*.

The honeysuckle and the climbing rose are supported on wires rather than trellis – the plants quickly scramble along the wires and cover them from view.

Sunny scented arbor

This planting provides a continuous display of flowers from late spring throughout the summer months until the frosts. The honeysuckle is the first to flower in late spring. The roses bloom in early summer, but with regular deadheading they could still be in flower until the fall. Lavender blooms in early summer and continues until the fall – although the scent fades with the color. White flowering tobacco plants peep over the the bench – but don't plant them until the frosts are over.

3 Honeysuckle (*Lonicera japonica* 'Halliana')

4 Rose (*Rosa* 'Golden Showers')

2 Flowering tobacco (*Nicotiana sylvestris*)

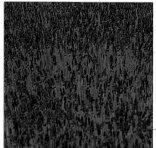

1 Lavender (*Lavandula angustifolia* 'Hidcote')

MAINTENANCE

• *Water regularly – especially during hot weather.*

• *Remove the rose flowers as they fade, as this will help to prolong the flowering season.*

• *In spring, snip off dead lavender flower heads and sprinkle some granular fertilizer around the base of the lavender plants.*

• *Keep the bed weeded. Mulch with compost or farmyard manure.*

• *Lift and discard the flowering tobacco in early fall. Plant new flowering tobacco in late spring once the frosts are over.*

PROJECT PLANNER

TIME SCALE **½ DAY**

Tools and Materials

Spirit level • Pencil or chalk • Electric drill and drill bit • Anchors • Hammer • Screwdriver • 2-in (5-cm) and 3-in (7.5-cm) screw eyes • $^1/_{10}$-in (2.5-mm) galvanized wire • Wire cutters • Pliers • Plastic-coated wire • Fork • Compost or garden manure • Rake • Wire ties

1 *Decide on the location for the bench, allowing space for a bed at either end. Mark the position of the wires on the wall, spacing the rows 18 in–2 ft (45–60 cm) apart. Mark the position of the screw eyes, positioning them along each row at intervals of approximately 18 in (45 cm). If possible, avoid putting them in mortar joints. At each end of each row, mark the position for a 2-in (5-cm) screw eye first, with a 3-in (7.5-cm) one 4–6 in (10–15 cm) in from the end of the row.*

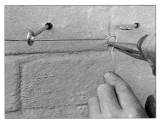

2 *Drill holes in the wall at the appropriate points and tap in an anchor.*

3 *Screw in a 2-in (5-cm) eye at each end of each row and at the center, and a 3-in (7.5-cm) eye 4–6 in (10–15 cm) further along the row.*

4 *Using a hammer, bend the 3-in (7.5-cm) screw eyes over so that they are about 45° from the vertical and leaning toward the center of the row.*

5 *Cut lengths of $^1/_{10}$-in (2.5-mm) galvanized wire, thread it through the screw eyes, and bend one end of the wire over to form a hook.*

6 *Pinching the bent end of the wire with the pliers to hold it firmly, bind the ends of the galvanized wire with plastic-coated wire.*

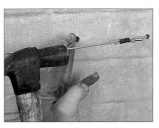

7 *Tighten the wire by hammering the angled screw eyes back until they are in a vertical position.*

8 *Prepare the bed at the foot of the wall and at either end of the bench (see page 46).*

9 *Buy the plants. If you can't plant them immediately, stand them in the shade and keep them watered.*

10 *Plant the plants (see pages 30–33). Attach the climber stems to the wires using wire ties.*

Adding Color to Green Hedges
FLOWERING CLEMATIS HEDGE

IF YOU WOULD LIKE to introduce some variety into an all-green hedge, plant a flowering climber alongside it to lift the sweep of clipped foliage and to create an unusual and attractive garden feature. There are many flowering climbing plants that respond well to being clipped along with your hedge. Annual climbers, such as sweet peas or morning glory, produce an attractive show of summer color. Alternatively, as here, you can make a permanent feature using a number of perennial climbers that flower at different times.

The clematis group of species, hybrids, and varieties — especially the less vigorous ones — are an excellent choice for growing through a hedge. They are strong but not very demanding feeders, so they can tolerate the often impoverished soil at the foot of a hedge. Their flowers and, if you put off clipping the hedge until late fall, their fluffy seedheads stand out well against most hedging plants, yet their foliage is unobtrusive. The late-flowering Viticella hybrids, such as the dark-pink *Clematis* 'Abundance', make an excellent choice for threading through a hedge.

Yellow and purple hedge flowers

If you choose your clematis carefully, you can have something in flower from spring until fall. Here the silky seedheads of spring-flowering blue Clematis alpina *'Frances Rivis' appear while the other clematis — a yellow* Clematis tangutica *and a purple* Clematis *'Jackmanii Superba' — are flowering. Leave hedge cutting until late in the year to get the best out of the clematis — or do it early in the year before the clematis starts flowering.*

1 *Clematis* 'Jackmanii Superba'

PLANTING ALTERNATIVES

Fiery patchwork hedge

Scarlet and green are opposites on the color spectrum and, when planted together, make a particularly vivid contrast. The plants listed below work extremely well against a fine-leaved conifer hedge. Flame nasturtium makes a spectacular splash of scarlet during the summer and the crimson glory vine turns yellow and scarlet in the fall. The large leaves of the crimson glory vine and the golden hop contrast especially well with fine-leaved conifer hedges. Golden hop has wonderful sharp green leaves with twining stems and green, hanging flowers in the fall.

1 Crimson glory vine (*Vitis coignetiae*)
2 Flame nasturtium (*Tropaeolum speciosum*)
3 Golden hop (*Humulus lupulus* 'Aureus')

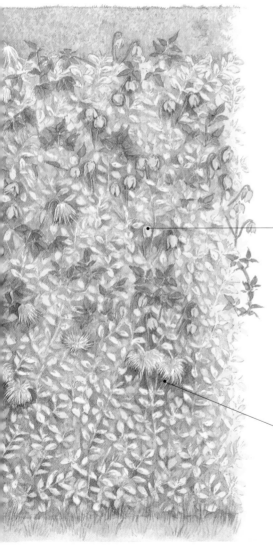

PROJECT PLANNER

TIME SCALE **½ DAY**

Tools and Materials

Hand fork • Hose or watering can • Spade • Manure or garden compost • Bone meal • Mulch
The time scale above is for 10 plants (1 per yd/m).

1 Buy the plants. If you can't plant immediately, keep them in the shade and water them daily.

2 Clear out the ground at the bottom of the hedge. Use a small hand fork to loosen the soil. If necessary, soften the soil with water before planting.

3 Carefully remove the stake that supports the clematis.

4 Dig a planting hole – clematis are best planted deeper than the level they were planted at in their pot – adding a soil improver to the hole (see page 33).

5 Intertwine the clematis stems through the branches of the hedge.

6 Water thoroughly and apply a mulch to conserve moisture – the soil at the base of a hedge is often dry and impoverished.

3 *Clematis tangutica*

MAINTENANCE

• *Cut the hedge in early spring, using sharp shears or a powered hedge cutter.*

• *Add a layer of manure or garden compost to the base of the hedge around the clematis plants each spring.*

2 *Clematis alpina* 'Frances Rivis', shown here in flower in early spring

A Garden Divider
POST-AND-CHAIN ROSE BOUNDARY

To MARK OFF an awkwardly shaped corner of the garden or to break up an over-wide expanse of lawn, use a procession of posts linked by chains swathed in climbing roses. A boundary such as this, where you can see between the upright posts, draws the eye to the plants and features that lie beyond and gives a much more open feel than a solid hedge or wall.

This divider makes a particularly successful support for roses, since they benefit from having air circulating through their branches. It proivdes the ideal opportunity to grow a favorite climbing rose – or even a collection of climbers. Traditionally, thick ropes would be used to link the uprights in this sort of design, but here, chain is used, as it is easier to hook on to the posts.

Pink rose boundary
Here the fabulous shell-pink rambler rose 'Albertine' clambers up the wooden posts and along the black chains. Smother the ground at the foot of the rose with lady's mantle to help diguise the bare stems of the rose and the metal casing at the base of the post.

1 *Rosa* 'Albertine'

MAINTENANCE

- *Remove aphids from young rose growth. Remove infested growth if necessary (see pages 36–37).*
- *Deadhead the roses as they fade.*
- *Trim the lady's mantle in summer to encourage fresh growth.*
- *Prune the roses in fall (see page 42).*
- *Mulch with compost after pruning.*

2 Lady's mantle
(*Alchemilla mollis*)

PROJECT PLANNER

TIME SCALE **1 DAY**

Tools and Materials

Garden twine • Metal rod • Spirit level • Metal post holders • Driving tool • 14-lb hammer • 8-ft (2.5-m) pretreated lumber posts • Screwdriver • 2-in (5-cm) hooks • 1–2-in (2.5–5-cm) chain • Step ladder • Post caps • Garden fork • Compost or manure

1 *Using garden twine, mark where the row of posts will go. Drive a metal rod into the ground, to the same depth as the post holder, as a pilot hole. Check that it is vertical with a spirit level. Repeat every 8–10 ft (2.5–3 m).*

2 *Remove the metal rod and insert a metal post holder into each pilot hole. Knock in the post holders using a 14-lb hammer.*

3 *Insert the posts into the holders. Knock them in firmly, using the 14-lb hammer (you may need to stand on a step ladder, getting someone else to hold it steady for you).*

4 *Position the rest of the posts and check that they are level with one another. Screw in the hooks 1–2 in (2.5–5 cm) below the top of each post.*

5 *Place the chain on the hooks and adjust the length of the chain to give the desired loop.*

6 *Fit decorative post caps. Nail the capping plate to the top of the post and screw on the finial.*

7 *Dig in compost or manure around the base of each post, then plant a rose at the base of each post (see page 33). Twine the stems around the posts. Plant lady's mantle at the foot of each rose.*

Informal Boundary Hedge
FLOWERING HEDGE

THERE ARE LOTS of good reasons for planting a hedge to mark a boundary rather than putting up a fence or wall. First, a hedge provides the best windbreak you can have: it allows some wind through, so no turbulence is created and the effect of the wind is reduced. Second, a hedge can screen your garden from the view of passersby or neighboring buildings. Last, but by no means least, a hedge is an excellent refuge and food source for wildlife.

If you have enough space, an informal hedge is often the best idea since informal hedges do not need to be clipped as often or as comprehensively as a formal, dense hedge. They also have a slightly rural look – as if your garden is at the edge of the countryside.

Choose a hedging plant that provides you with a screen throughout the year. It need not be evergreen but it should be dense and bushy. Also choose something with at least two seasons of interest – flowers followed by berries, for example. Alternatively, plant a mixed hedge with several different species; local wildlife will enjoy this kind of hedge best of all.

Purple flowering hedge

Rosa rugosa makes a dense and attractive hedge all year round, from spring when its crinkled leaves emerge, through its purple-pink flowers in mid-summer, and large red hips in the fall and beyond. It has prickly stems and is a great deterrent to potential trespassers.

PLANTING ALTERNATIVES

Evergreen, yellow-berried hedge

Firethorns are among the most useful hedging plants –
especially if an impenetrable hedge is required. They are
evergreen plants, with creamy white blossom in spring.
'Saphyr Jaune' makes a dense, disease-free hedge with
bright yellow berries, but there are many other varieties of
firethorn to choose from with red, yellow, or orange berries
that last from the fall through the winter months.

Firethorn (*Pyracantha* 'Saphyr Jaune')

Fast-growing evergreen hedge

Conifers are an extremely popular choice if you want a
fast-growing hedge. However, speed of growth is a double-
edged sword as far as hedges go since the quicker a plant
grows, the more it needs clipping. Many popular conifers
are much too vigorous for hedging, though they are often
sold as suitable hedging plants. Leyland cypress, for example, is much too fast-growing for a hedge – especially in a
small garden – and requires frequent clipping to keep it
within bounds. If you want a fast-growing conifer hedge,
choose the more manageable Lawson's cypress.

Lawson's cypress (*Chamaecyparis lawsoniana*)

Rosa rugosa

PROJECT PLANNER

TIME SCALE 1 DAY

Tools and Materials

Rope or twine and pegs • Yardstick
• Fork • Spade • Manure or garden
compost • Bone meal • Pruning shears
*The time scale above is for a hedge
about 20 ft (7 m) long.*

1 *Decide on the location of the hedge. Position cardboard
boxes at the height the hedge will reach when fully
grown. This will show you what the hedge will hide from
view once it is mature. It will also give you an idea of how
much shelter the hedge will give from prevailing wind, and
of how long and dense a shadow it will cast at different
times of day.*

2 *Mark out the line of the hedge (see page 32) and calculate how many plants you need.*

3 *Buy the hedging plants. If you buy bare-rooted plants,
soak them for several hours before planting. If you buy
containerized plants and can't plant them immediately, keep
them watered and in the shade.*

4 *Prepare the site and plant the hedge (see page 32).*

5 *After planting, water the hedge thoroughly. Apply a
2–3-in (5–7.5-cm) layer of manure or garden compost
as a mulch. If you are planting in warm, dry weather, don't
allow the soil to dry out – especially in the first few weeks
after planting.*

6 *Trim back the newly planted hedge by one third all the
way around (see page 44). If your site is exposed, use
windbreak netting to protect the hedge for the first season.*

MAINTENANCE

• *Keep the hedge bottom free of weeds by regular hoeing.*

• *Water regularly – especially during dry weather in the
first summer.*

• *In spring, once the soil has warmed up, apply a 2–3-in
(5–7.5-cm) layer of garden compost or manure to the soil
around the plants.*

• *Clip the hedge in late summer each year – or, if it
bears fruits in the fall, in early spring before the birds
start nesting. Use sharp shears or a powered hedge trimmer.*

Formal Hedge
A GARDEN WITHIN A GARDEN

HEDGES DO NOT ALWAYS mark the external boundary of your garden. A formal clipped hedge is a simple, but extremely effective way of dividing a large garden into smaller, more intimate sections. Plant alleyways of hedges to intrigue visitors and tempt them to walk down them to see what is there; alternatively, as in the design shown below, use the hedge to form a garden within your garden – a natural "room" where you can sit in seclusion.

A formal hedge makes an ideal backdrop for beds and borders of plants; the plain color and straight, flat surfaces contrast and set off the irregular shapes and shadows of the plants in front. There are many different types of hedging plants to choose from. Quick-growing conifers and slower-growing beech are just two of the options open to you. Conifers, with finely divided evergreen foliage, make a smooth-textured hedge. However, you should avoid the fast-growing varieties unless you quickly need a windbreak. Beech makes a beautiful fresh green hedge that grows to the height of 5 ft (1.5 m) within 5 years. Although it is not an evergreen, it keeps its dead leaves in winter; they turn a russetty brown that warms up the garden in the coldest months.

To make hedge cutting easier and to make your bed or border plants stand out even more, it is a good idea to lay a path between the hedge and the back of the border. It need not be visible from the front of the border or bed so it can be made from concrete slabs bedded on coarse sand.

Green backdrop

Here a handsome green beech hedge provides a lively but neutral background to a border of shrubs and perennials.

PLANTING ALTERNATIVES

Purple shadows

Instead of bright green, choose a dark, red-leaved beech variety that makes a dramatic contrast behind a bed or border of perennials and shrubs.

Purple beech (*Fagus sylvatica* Atropurpurea Group)

Velvety conifer

The king of conifer hedges is the slow-growing, velvety-looking yew. It may take time to reach the height you want – 5 years or more to reach 5 ft (1.5 m) – but it stays much neater than a fast-growing conifer and does not need as much clipping.

Yew (*Taxus baccata*)

Beech (*Fagus sylvatica*)

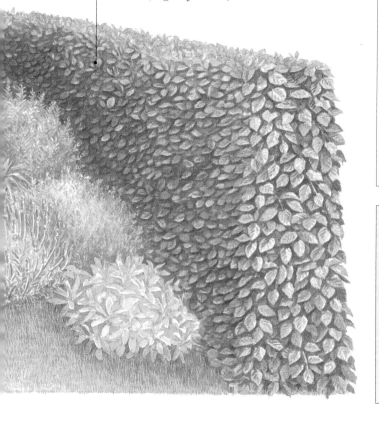

PROJECT PLANNER

TIME SCALE **1 DAY**

Tools and Materials

Garden twine or rope and pegs • Yardstick • Watering can or hose • Fork • Spade • Manure or garden compost • Bone meal • Pruning shears • Paving slabs • Coarse sand • Spirit level
The time scale above is for a hedge about 20 ft (7 m) long.

1 *Decide on the location of the hedge. Position cardboard boxes at the height the hedge will reach when fully grown. This will show you what the hedge will hide from view once it is mature. It will also give you an idea of how much shelter the hedge will give from prevailing wind, and of how long and dense a shadow it will cast at different times of day.*

2 *Mark the line of the hedge and calculate how many plants you need (see page 32).*

3 *Buy the hedging plants. If you buy bare-rooted plants, soak them for several hours before planting. If you buy containerized plants and can't plant them immediately, keep them watered and in the shade.*

4 *Prepare the site and plant the hedge (see page 32).*

5 *Water thoroughly. Apply a 2–3-in (5–7.5-cm) layer of manure or garden compost to the soil at the bottom of the hedge as a mulch after watering.*

6 *Trim back the newly planted hedge by one third all the way around (see page 44).*

7 *Lay the maintenance-path paving slabs parallel to the hedge. Remove the top 4 in (10 cm) of soil, put down a 2-in (5-cm) layer of coarse sand, then lay down the paving slab. Use a spirit level to check that it is level in every direction before you lay the next slab.*

8 *Create and plant a bed in front of the maintenance path (see page 46).*

MAINTENANCE

• *Keep the hedge bottom free of weeds by regular hoeing.*

• *Water regularly – especially during dry weather in the first summer.*

• *In spring, once the soil has warmed up, apply a 2–3-in (5–7.5-cm) layer of compost or manure to the soil around the plants.*

• *Clip your hedge in late summer each year using sharp shears or a powered hedge trimmer (see page 44).*

Defining Your Beds
MINIATURE HEDGING

FOR WELL-DEFINED beds and a stylish-looking garden, edge your beds with dwarf hedging. Uniform edging can transform a random grouping of plants into a coherent unit – similar to framing a picture.

Like regular-sized hedging, miniature hedges can be either formal or informal, depending on the type of hedging plant you choose. For a neat, dark, evergreen line around your beds, box (*Buxus sempervirens* 'Suffruticosa') is very effective. Its tiny leaves give a uniform appearance and its relatively slow growth rate means that clipping is limited to two or three times per summer, ideal for the weekend gardener. For a more relaxed feel, lavender is a colorful, eye-catching way of setting off a plain, upright planting more than 2 ft (60 cm) high. Choose a compact variety, such as 'Hidcote', which has dark purple flowers.

You can even make a feature that uses miniature hedging plants exclusively, arranging them in a geometric pattern in the same way as traditional "knot gardens" as in the design below. This is a particularly good idea if you're planting something that will be seen from above – from an upper apartment window, for example. You can use two, three, or more hedging species with contrasting colors and textures. The only point to consider is the ease of maintenance – make sure you can clip and weed easily or the neatness of the effect will quickly be lost.

Dark green crisscross with lavender

Here a crisscross pattern of box 9-in (22.5-cm) high is framed by a taller 1-ft (30-cm) high hedge of the same plant. A single lavender plant sits in each square, its upright spikiness contrasting dramatically with the horizontal planes of the hedging. The central bay tree ball (potted so that it can be brought indoors in the coldest weather) presents another contrasting form.

PLANTING ALTERNATIVES

Dark green crisscross with yellow

Use a yellow-flowered lemon verbena, grown as a standard, in place of the bay and cotton lavender, with its delicate yellow flowers in place of the lavender.

1 Lemon verbena *(Aloysia triphylla)*

2 Cotton lavender *(Santolina chamaecyparissus)*

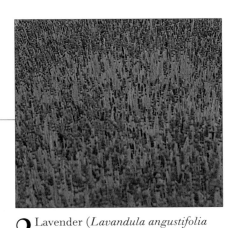

1 Bay *(Laurus nobilis)*

2 Lavender *(Lavandula angustifolia 'Hidcote')*

3 Box *(Buxus sempervirens)*

PROJECT PLANNER

TIME SCALE **1 DAY**

Tools and Materials

Pencil and graph paper • Yardstick • Stakes • Watering can or hose • Spade • Fork • Manure or garden compost • Bone meal • Gravel or bark-chip mulch • Pruning shears *The time scale above is for a site about 10 yd (10 m) long.*

1 *Decide on the pattern you want for your miniature hedging and draw it on graph paper.*

2 *Referring to your plan, measure the site with a yardstick. Mark the line of the hedge with stakes every yard (meter) or more and calculate how many plants you need.*

3 *Buy the hedging plants. If you buy bare-rooted plants, soak them for several hours before planting. If you buy containerized plants and can't plant them immediately, keep them watered and in the shade.*

4 *Prepare the site and plant the plants (see page 32). For a miniature hedge, a trench 1 ft (30 cm) wide and 10–12 in (25–30 cm) deep is big enough.*

5 *Water well and mulch around the base of the trench with gravel or bark.*

6 *Trim back the sides of the hedging plants by one third after planting, leaving the top intact until the desired height is reached (see page 44).*

7 *Mulch around the lavender plants with manure or garden compost.*

MAINTENANCE

• *Keep the bed well watered and weeded.*

• *In the fall, water the bed well and replenish the mulch..*

• *Clip the hedge twice each summer.*

• *Trim lavender in spring and again after the flowers have faded.*

• *Clip the bay in summer and move it indoors in the fall before the first frosts.*

Front-yard Boundary
PICKET FENCES

ANEAT AND FRESHLY PAINTED front-yard fence sets your house and garden off to its best advantage. Picket fencing is both inexpensive to buy and easy to erect. You can make your own or buy ready-made panels – in which case all you have to do is supply the posts to support the panels and paint the fence your chosen color. Plant tall flowers, such as lupins, delphiniums, and hollyhocks, along the inside of the fence for a nostalgic cottage-garden look.

Picket fences are available in many different designs. The tops of the slats can be rounded in shape, pointed, intricately carved, or pierced. You can have slats that graduate in height, so that the fence looks curved or wavy. You can even change the material and use bamboo canes instead of wooden slats.

The width of the slats and how far apart you space them is up to you. Before you start to assemble the fence, draw your design on graph paper so that you can caluclate how many slats you will need.

Picket fences don't last for ever, so check them regularly, clean them, replace any broken or rotten slats, and repaint every 2–3 years to keep them looking fresh.

Unique fencing

Devise your own slat shape and draw the design on graph paper. Get your local lumber yard to cut the slats to size, following your pattern. Order more than you need so that you have some spare.

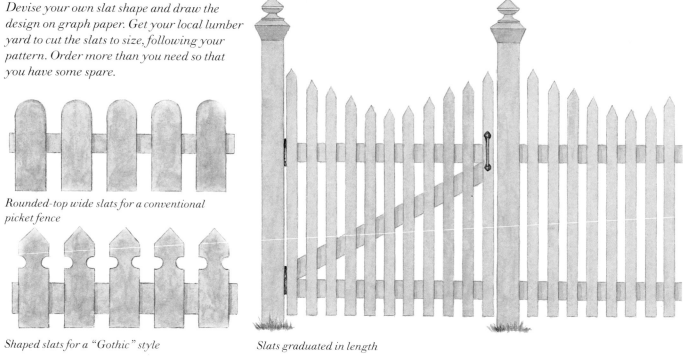

Rounded-top wide slats for a conventional picket fence

Shaped slats for a "Gothic" style

Slats graduated in length

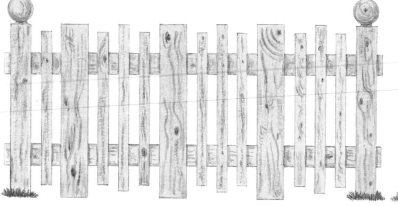

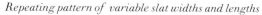

Repeating pattern of variable slat widths and lengths

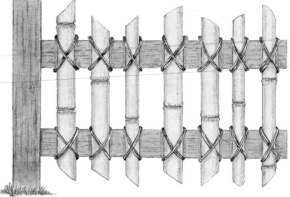

Bamboo picket fence with canes

118

PROJECT PLANNER

TIME SCALE

1 DAY

Tools and Materials

Screwdriver • 2-in (5-cm) screws • Pretreated lumber gate with hinges and catch fittings • Pretreated lumber gate posts • Metal rod • Metal post holders • Post driving tool • 14-lb hammer • Spirit level • Slotted fence posts and rails • Garden twine • Fence slats or panels of ready-made picket fence • Nails • Mallet • Exterior wood paint and paint bush
The time scale given above is for a fence about 10 yd (10 m) long.

1 *Screw hinges and catch fittings to gate and posts. Using the rod, make a hole and insert a post holder every 3–4 yds (3–4 m). Hammer posts into holders, covering with the driving tool for protection.*

2 *Position the gate between the gate posts (ask a friend to help you). Shut the gate and check that it is level and that the catch closes correctly.*

3 *Run garden twine along the top of the fence and use this as a guide-line for where the top of the slats should be. Slot the fence rails into the fence posts, then check that the fence framework is level.*

4 *Nail the slats to the rails. Ask your helper to push firmly against the rail on the opposite side with a mallet while you hammer in the nail. Put two nails in the top rail and two in the bottom.*

5 *Continue to nail in the slats, checking the levels constantly and making sure they are the correct distance apart. Paint the fence with your chosen finish.*

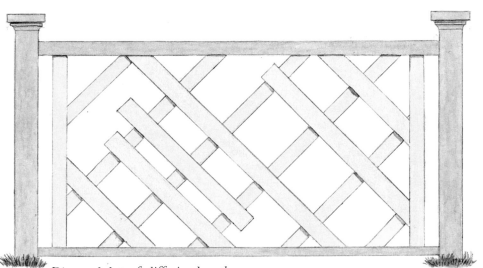

Diagonal slats of differing lengths

MAINTENANCE

• *Check the fence and gate posts every year to make sure they are still firm. If they become wobbly, you may need to reset them in concrete.*

• *Repaint the fence and gate every 2–3 years.*

BEDS AND BORDERS

Glorious color
From the bushy, yellow daisy flowers of helenium in the foreground to the dramatic, spikes of orange crocosmia in the distance, this splendid border of red and gold perennial flowers makes an impressive splash of color and provides a dramatic focal point to the garden.

Ideas for Sunny Beds and Borders

BEDS AND BORDERS in sunny situations allow you to grow flowers in abundance. Many of the perennials that form the mainstay of herbaceous borders are sun-loving species. If your garden gets the sun, you will be able to grow these wonderful flowers year after year for their stunning colors and intoxicating fragrance.

However, you must select plants that actually enjoy direct sun: moisture-loving species can survive in sunny spots – but only if you're willing to devote much of your valuable weekend time to watering them. Any good plant manual will give you this information. Study the label accompanying the potted plant before you buy. You'll be making life easier for yourself, since happy plants require less maintenance.

The questions on these two pages are designed to help you pinpoint ways in which you can improve shaded beds and borders. Each one is backed up by a step-by-step project with plants that have been specifically chosen because they thrive in sunny spots.

? *Do you have a sun-baked area where plants often wilt ?*

Not all sun-loving plants thrive in very hot situations. Choose plants that really enjoy sun to reduce the amount of watering required. *Right*: Golden genista lydia, a euphorbia, ornamental onions, gray-leaved sedum, stripy century plant, and ground-smothering lamb's ears are all suitable.
SEE *Bed for a Hot, Dry Site, page 124*.

? *Does your garden lack interest at certain times of year?*

Make sure there is always something interesting to look at – spring-flowering bulbs, fall hips, evergreens, and plants with interesting winter bark all help to give a garden year-round visual appeal.
SEE *Planting for Year-round Interest, page 134*.

? *Do you like rich, hot colors?*

Many herbaceous perennials like sunny sites and have hot-colored flowers (red, gold, orange). They bloom year after year and require relatively little maintenance.
SEE *Emphasizing a Sunny Site, page 132*.

? *Does your garden lack a focal point?*

An arbor or archway, smothered in blooms, makes an eye-catching feature. *Right:* Here, the rambler rose, *Rosa* 'Félicité Perpétue' makes a marvellous colorful spectacle. Rosemary clothes the base of the archway.
SEE *Creating a Focal Point, page 130.*

? *Is there bare earth around new shrubs?*

Bushes and shrubs can take several years to reach their full height and spread. Fill in the gaps with annual flowers that you've grown from seed. *Above:* In this border, yellow daisies, orange tickseed, and tall white cosmos make a colorful display between the permanent plants.
SEE *Filling Gaps in Borders, page 128.*

? *Do you have a low border where the plants are of similar height?*

Introduce a taller feature, such as a sweet-pea tower, for visual variety.
SEE *Creating Height in a Border, page 126.*

Bed for a Hot, Dry Site

FIERY LANDSCAPE

GIVE YOUR GARDEN the feeling of an oasis in an arid landscape by creating a bed for dry-soil plants. Sheltered, sunny areas lend themselves to recreating a semidesert scene, especially if the soil is well drained. Check the soil to make sure that water drains away quickly; you may need to dig in horticultural sand or fine gravel to improve the drainage (see page 19).

Dome the bed slightly so that the soil is higher in the middle and set feature rocks into the slope. Natural semidesert habitats tend to be barren and rocky. By incorporating rocks in the bed you will create a natural, authentic-looking setting.

After planting, cover the soil with pebbles and gravel to create a natural-looking "scree" landscape.

8 Mount Etna broom (*Genista aetnensis*)

Blaze of color

The planting in this bed gives a dramatic appearance. Fiery hues of red, yellow, and orange predominate, while contrasts in form, height, and texture give extra interest.

1 Myrtle euphorbia (*Euphorbia myrsinites*)

2 *Yucca gloriosa*

3 Evening primrose (*Oenothera fruticosa* 'Fireworks')

4 Wood millet (*Milium effusum* 'Aureum')

7 California poppy
(*Eschscholzia californica*)

6 Dwarf juniper (*Juniperus communis* 'Compressa')

5 Cypress spurge
(*Euphorbia cyparissias*)

PROJECT PLANNER

Tools and Materials

TIME SCALE 1 DAY

Fork • Rake • Horticultural grit or fine gravel • Large rocks • Tree stake and ties • Trowel • Pebble or gravel mulch
The time scale above is for a site about 10 x 5 ft (3 x 1.5 m).

1 *Mark out the site and prepare the soil (see page 46), adding plenty of horticultural sand or fine gravel if the soil is not sandy to improve drainage.*

2 *Buy some large rocks (or move them from other areas of the garden) and set them in position. They should be set into the ground so that they look natural.*

3 *Buy the plants. If you cannot plant them immediately, store them in a cool place and keep well watered.*

4 *Position the plants around the bed. Once you are happy with their placement, plant them. Plant and stake the Mount Etna broom first, and then plant the yucca, dwarf junipers, and wood millet. Finally, plant the small plants — the evening primroses, California poppies, Cypress spurge, and myrtle euphorbia.*

5 *Water thoroughly. Cover any exposed soil in pebbles or gravel to act as a mulch and create a natural-looking scree landscape.*

MAINTENANCE

• *Keep the bed weeded, especially in the first two seasons while plants are establishing themselves. Allow a few clumps of California poppy seedlings to remain.*

• *Cut back dead, straggly, or unwanted growth in the fall.*

• *Deadhead flowers of all plants once they are past their best to help keep the bed tidy and to encourage a second flush of flowers.*

• *Plant spring-flowering bulbs such as crocuses or irises in the fall.*

• *Replenish the pebble or gravel mulch in late spring to help suppress weed growth.*

Creating Height in a Border

SWEET-PEA TOWER

BOTH NEWLY planted and well-established gardens can benefit from the introduction of a feature that provides height and scale. A bed that contains nothing but low-growing plants can sometimes look monotonous, and a tall stucture provides a much-needed focal point. For a permanent feature, you can buy an upright garden statue and train plants to grow over it, or you can use a tall, attractive plant support made of metal, cane, or wattle. However, if you want just a temporary feature to bring some height to a bed of young plants, then a home-made bamboo tower is an attractive solution. Ideal plants for growing in this way are annual climbers such as morning glory, canary creeper, and black-eyed Susan. In a matter of weeks you can have a magnificent display of flowers and foliage that will last through the summer and fall.

PLANTING ALTERNATIVES

Single-color cascade

A number of annual climbers can be grown in the same way as the sweet-pea tower. The plants listed below offer a range of color schemes.

Morning glory
(*Ipomoea rubrocaerulea* 'Heavenly Blue')
– blue flowers

Canary creeper
(*Tropaeolum peregrinum*)
– yellow flowers

Black-eyed Susan
(*Thunbergia alata*)
– orange flowers

Mixed-color cascade

Sweet peas are ideal subjects for training up bamboo stakes at the back of a bed. A tall-growing variety will quickly clamber up to create an eye-catching cascade – and the more blooms you pick the more they produce, so you can fill your house with their delicious scent as a bonus.

1 Sweet pea (*Lathyrus odoratus* 'Galaxy Mixed')

MAINTENANCE

• *A week or so after the sweet peas are planted, pinch out all but the strongest shoot on each seedling.*

• *Use a wire ring to hold the seedling loosely against the stake. Tendrils will soon grow and cling firmly to the support.*

• *Keep the area free of weeds and water regularly.*

• *Deadhead every few days to keep flowers coming, or pick fresh flowers for the house.*

• *Apply a liquid fertilizer once flowering is established.*

PLANTING ALTERNATIVES

Tasty towers

As an alternative to flowers, there are a number of vegetable crops that can be grown on stakes. All the varieties listed below produce attractive flowers as well as vegetables.

Runner bean (*Phaseolus coccineus* 'Painted Lady') – red and white flowers

Pea (*Pisum sativum* 'Carouby de Maussane') – purple flowers

Pumpkin (*Cucurbita pepo* 'Munchkin') – yellow flowers

PROJECT PLANNER

TIME SCALE 1 HOUR

Tools and Materials

Rake • 8 bamboo stakes, 6–7 ft (1.8–2.1 m) tall • Garden twine, string, or raffia • Trowel • Wire rings

1 *Sow sweet peas in a pot or tray indoors in fall or early spring (see page 29)*

2 *At least two weeks before planting, prepare the ground by turning the earth just as you would if you were creating a new bed (see page 46). Break up any large clumps of soil and rake the surface smooth.*

3 *Arrange the eight bamboo stakes in a circle approximately 3 ft (1 m) in diameter. Insert them firmly into the soil so that they are all the same height.*

4 *Gather the tops of the stakes together in your hand and bind them securely with garden twine, string, or raffia.*

5 *Using the same twine, secure the stakes about 3 ft (1 m) from the ground. This will help to stabilize the structure as well as give the growing plants something horizontal to cling on to.*

6 *When the sweet pea seedlings are at least 2 in (5 cm) tall, water them, remove from their containers, and gently separate them. Plant a single seedling at the base of each stake.*

Filling Gaps in Borders
PINK AND WHITE PLANTING

IF YOU HAVE GAPS between permanent plants, such as shrubs, why not fill them with a display of colorful summer annuals? As annuals last for only one year, they are not permanent additions to your garden and there is no risk of them crowding out the shrubs. Covering bare ground with plants is also a good way of preventing weeds from growing. You can buy or grow your own annuals, choosing from the range of bedding plants available at garden centers or nurseries. If the choice at your local garden center is limited, order through seed catalogs.

Although it is time consuming to grow annuals from seed, it is also satisfying and much less expensive than buying established plants – and it is sometimes easier to find the exact varieties and flower colors that you want. Hardy annuals, such as those shown below, are the easiest plants to grow from seed. Sow them where you want them to flower, then thin out the seedlings when they are large enough to handle to give the others space in which to grow. Half-hardy plants are best raised in trays indoors so that the seedlings are ready to plant outside when the frosty weather is over.

Delicate pink and white

The front of a shrub border can look dull and lifeless even in summer. Here, home-raised hardy annuals are mixed with some bought-in half-hardy balsam plants to create a carpet of white and pink flowers.

PLANTING ALTERNATIVES

Creating a warm glow

For a warm display of predominantly orange and yellow flowers, substitute the plants listed below for those shown in the illustration.

1 Nasturtium
   (*Tropaeolum majus* 'Alaska')

3 Poached-egg flower
   (*Limnanthes douglasii*)

4 Pot marigold
   (*Calendula officinalis*)

1 Balsam (*Impatiens balsamina*)

2 Sweet alyssum
(*Lobularia maritima*)

4 Snapdragon (*Antirrhinum* '*White Wonder*')

3 Candytuft (*Iberis amara*)

PROJECT PLANNER

TIME SCALE 1 HOUR

Tools and Materials

Fork • Rake • Stick • Sand • Chicken wire • Plant labels • Old kitchen fork

1 *Identify the gaps you want to fill. Remove any weeds and fork over the soil. Rake it smooth.*

2 *If you are growing the hardy annuals from seed, sow the seeds where you want them to flower (see page 29). Label them and protect them from cats and birds with chicken wire. When they are large enough to handle, thin them out using an old kitchen fork. If you are buying the plants, be sure to harden them off before you plant them; leave them outside during the day but bring them indoors at night until all danger of frost has passed.*

MAINTENANCE

• *After thinning out seedlings to allow enough room for the remaining plants to develop, check the area frequently for weeds, slugs, and other pests and remove them as they appear.*

• *Water frequently, particularly in dry weather.*

• *Pinch off the tips of snapdragon seedlings to create bushier plants.*

• *Remove spent flower stems to encourage more flowers to develop.*

129

Creating a Focal Point
SCENTED LILY AND ROSE ARBOR

A FREE-STANDING ARBOR or arch swathed in flowers brings several benefits to a garden: it can be used to divide the garden into separate areas, to frame a striking view, or to distract attention from an unattractive one. Beyond these, it provides a focal point – a dramatic, eye-catching feature that makes a strong design statement.

You can make your own arch, but it is far easier to buy one in kit form from a garden center. There is a wide range to choose from – in wood and metal – and to suit all budgets. Once you have made sure that the arch is well anchored in the ground, you can start to train climbing plants to grow up and around it.

An arch is a particularly effective way of displaying such scented climbers as roses or honeysuckle, since you benefit from wafts of perfume every time you pass through it. Some rose varieties, particularly if they are trained over a wall or solid surface, are prone to mildew in humid conditions. However, growing them over an arch can help prevent this problem, since air is able to circulate freely through the plants' stems.

Fragrant pink and white arch
This arch is smothered in fragrant pink roses, while pots of lilies clothe the base. Geraniums and sweet violets cover the ground and help to minimize weed growth.

1 Pink rambler rose such as *Rosa* 'New Dawn'

2 Madonna lily (*Lilium candidum*)

3 Pink climbing rose such as *Rosa* 'Zéphirine Drouhin'

4 *Geranium* x *magnificum*

5 Sweet violet (*Viola odorata*), shown here in flower in spring

MAINTENANCE

- *Weed regularly.*

- *Water regularly, especially in warm and dry weather.*

- *In spring, sprinkle fertilizer around the base of the rose plants.*

- *Use old panty hose to tie the stems of the climbing rose to the arch. Wind the plant stems around the arch as they grow.*

- *Deadhead roses as they fade, snipping off their stems to just above a vigorous leaf joint.*

- *Prune Rosa 'New Dawn' after it has flowered. Unwind the stems and cut each one that has flowered back to its main stem (see page 42). The other rose used here (Rosa 'Zéphirine Drouhin') is a climber and need not be pruned regularly, though unwanted or dead stems can be removed in spring.*

- *Remove the pots of lilies once their flowers are over and replace them with pots of other flowering plants.*

- *In fall, remove dead leaves and other debris, and apply a mulch of bark chippings to the soil.*

PLANTING ALTERNATIVES

Golden arch

For a predominantly gold- and cream-colored planting scheme, substitute the plants listed below for those shown in the illustration.

1 *Rosa* 'Golden Showers'

3 *Rosa* 'Madame Alfred Carrière'

4 Lady's mantle (*Alchemilla mollis*)

5 Heartsease (*Viola tricolor*)

PROJECT PLANNER

TIME SCALE **1 DAY**

Tools and Materials

Arch kit • Post holders • Driving tool for post holders • 14-lb hammer • Mallet • Spirit level • Fork • Manure • Spade • Bark-chip mulch

1 *Decide where to position your archway. Measure your site roughly so that you can make (or buy) an appropriately sized archway.*

2 *Assemble the sides and top of the archway following the manufacturer's instructions.*

3 *Insert the first metal post holder into the ground. Fit the driving tool over the post holder and use the 14-lb hammer to knock the holder into position.*

4 *Lay one side panel on the ground to help you check where the second post should be positioned. Drive the second post holder into the ground in the same way as the first one.*

5 *Insert the first side panel into its post holders, knocking it in with a mallet. Lay a crossbar on the ground to help you position the post holders for the second side panel and insert the post holders as in Steps 3 and 4.*

6 *Insert the second side panel into its post holders, as in Step 5. Use a spirit level to check that the tops of the two side panels are level with each other, tapping them with the mallet if necessary.*

7 *Fit the overhead crosspieces into position. Check that they are level. Make any necessary adjustments by tapping them with the mallet.*

8 *Fork over the soil around the archway, incorporating manure so that the ground is well prepared before you plant.*

9 *Plant one rose at each side of the archway. Plant geraniums and violas around the base of the archway for ground cover.*

10 *Water well and cover the soil with a layer of bark chippings.*

11 *Position a container of Madonna lilies on each side of the archway.*

Emphasizing a Sunny Site
PERENNIALS IN SCARLET AND GOLD

PERENNIALS ARE the mainstay of the herbaceous border: they flower year after year and, unlike summer bedding plants and many bulbs, which need to be lifted after they have flowered and replaced the next year, they can be left permanently in place – a far easier proposition for the weekend gardener!

Many of the most popular and attractive perennials, including the ones shown below, thrive in full sun, so if you are fortunate enough to have a sunny area in your garden, make the most of it. Choose warm-colored plants to match the warm temperature – orange, scarlet, gold, and bright yellow. Nothing can beat a border of these often colorful and dramatic plants. If you choose your species carefully, you can have a continuous display of flowering plants from late spring until the fall.

Summer celebration

Enjoy the sunshine and warmth of summer with this scarlet and purple border, shown here in late summer. Bold clumps of red hot pokers, sneezeweed, crocosmia, daylilies, and dahlias are set off by plants with a softer form, such as geraniums, lady's mantle, and mountain bluet. Spilling over the front of the bed is a miniature hedge of catmint.

1 Red hot poker
(*Kniphofia* 'Alcazar')

2 Catmint
(*Nepeta* x *faassenii*)

3 Lady's mantle
(*Alchemilla mollis*)

4 *Geranium*
'Johnson's Blue'

5 Sneezeweed (*Helenium*
'Moerheim Beauty')

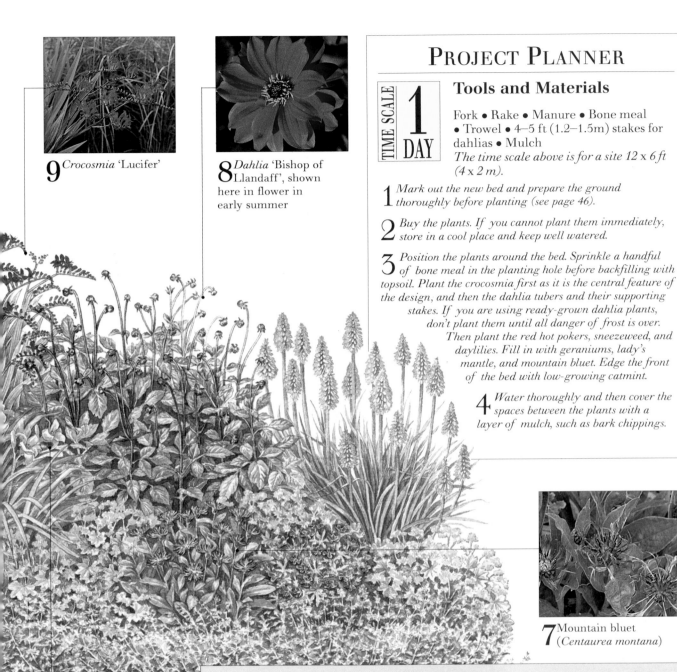

9 *Crocosmia* 'Lucifer'

8 *Dahlia* 'Bishop of Llandaff', shown here in flower in early summer

PROJECT PLANNER

TIME SCALE
1 DAY

Tools and Materials

Fork • Rake • Manure • Bone meal • Trowel • 4–5 ft (1.2–1.5m) stakes for dahlias • Mulch
The time scale above is for a site 12 x 6 ft (4 x 2 m).

1 *Mark out the new bed and prepare the ground thoroughly before planting (see page 46).*

2 *Buy the plants. If you cannot plant them immediately, store in a cool place and keep well watered.*

3 *Position the plants around the bed. Sprinkle a handful of bone meal in the planting hole before backfilling with topsoil. Plant the crocosmia first as it is the central feature of the design, and then the dahlia tubers and their supporting stakes. If you are using ready-grown dahlia plants, don't plant them until all danger of frost is over. Then plant the red hot pokers, sneezeweed, and daylilies. Fill in with geraniums, lady's mantle, and mountain bluet. Edge the front of the bed with low-growing catmint.*

4 *Water thoroughly and then cover the spaces between the plants with a layer of mulch, such as bark chippings.*

7 Mountain bluet (*Centaurea montana*)

MAINTENANCE

• *For bushy dahlias, pinch back growing tips of plants when they are about 12–18 in (30–45 cm) tall. For bigger flowers, pinch out some buds, leaving about 10 to develop. Feed with granular or liquid fertilizer in early summer.*

• *In summer, clip back any dead flowers and tired leaves to encourage fresh growth and flowers.*

• *Mulch the bed in the fall or late spring.*

• *Weed regularly and water in hot weather.*

• *Support dahlias and other tall perennials. Insert stakes or wire supports around each plant when it is about 12 in (30 cm) tall. Tie the stakes together to provide a framework through which the stems can grow.*

• *When frosts have killed the dahlia leaves, cut the stems about back to 6 in (15 cm). Lift the tubers and leave them to dry in a frost-free shed for 2–3 weeks. Pack them in peat or moss and store in a box over winter.*

• *Cut back the dead growth of other perennials in the fall (see page 39).*

6 Daylily (*Hemerocallis* 'Stella de Oro')

Planting for Year-round Interest

FOUR-SEASON ISLAND BED

IN MANY SITUATIONS it is important for a flower bed or border to look its best throughout the year. Choose plants that have different seasons of interest so that there is always something attractive to look at. Spring-flowering bulbs are a good choice for brightening up the early months of the year before the leaves of other plants emerge. If space is limited, use plants that have more than one season of interest – perhaps a spring-flowering shrub that also has attractive berries in fall. There are shrubs, such as some dogwoods and willows, that have dramatic, brightly colored stems in winter and spring if you prune them back each year.

Late-summer splendor

A hazel tree gives height to this island bed, but it also has yellow catkins in spring and medium-green leaves in summer turning to yellow in fall. Ground-cover plants and small bulbs provide a changing focus from season to season.

1 Hazel (*Corylus avellana*)

2 Snowdrop (*Galanthus* sp.); buy and plant new plants in spring, after flowering but before the leaves die back

3 *Nerine bowdenii* (plant bulbs in the fall)

4 Irish ivy (*Hedera hibernica*)

5 *Berberis thunbergii* 'Atropurpurea Nana'

9 Dogwood (*Cornus alba* 'Sibirica'), shown here in winter when its bright red stems are seen to best effect

8 Bistort (*Persicaria bistorta* 'Superba')

7 *Cyclamen coum* (plant tubers in the fall)

6 Winter iris (*Iris unguicularis*)

PROJECT PLANNER

TIME SCALE 1 DAY

Tools and Materials

• Garden hose or rope • Fork • Spade • Rake • Bone meal • Manure • Tree stake and ties • Fine soil • Bark-chip mulch
The time scale above is for a site about 12 x 6 ft (4 x 2 m).

1 Mark out the shape of the bed with a garden hose or some rope (see page 46).

2 Make the new bed, preparing the ground thoroughly (see page 46).

3 Buy the plants. Store in a cool place and keep well watered until you plant them.

4 Plant and stake the hazel tree (see page 33), and then plant the dogwood, berberis, and bistort. Spread the ivy stems over the ground and cover them with soil every 10–12 in (25–30 cm). Plant the cyclamen, snowdrops, and winter irises in the fall, covering the bulbs with fine soil. Plant the nerines in early fall or spring; the top of the bulb should just break the soil surface.

5 After planting, water thoroughly. Cover any exposed soil with a mulch of bark chippings.

MAINTENANCE

• Cut back the dogwood to just above ground level each spring. In summer, if it overshadows the iris clump, trim it back.

• Weed regularly and mulch in fall or late spring. Once plants are established weeding will be greatly reduced, since ground-cover plants are a feature of this design.

• Lift and divide the winter iris rhizomes in summer or early fall (see page 39).

Ideas for Shaded Beds and Borders

FLOWER BEDS AND borders in a shaded situation will never be quite as colorful as those in full sun, but you can still enjoy a rich and varied range of flowers and greenery. Use cool colors – blues, purples, greens – to create a tranquil, relaxing feel.

There are also some simple ways of creating the illusion that more light reaches the area than is actually the case: plant pale-colored flowers to accentuate what little light there is, paint neighboring walls a light color, or position a mirror to reflect light outward. The plants you choose can help, too: small, feathery-leaved plants are better than large, solid-looking species as they give a lighter, less dense overall effect.

The questions on these two pages are designed to help you pinpoint ways in which you can improve shaded beds and borders. Each one is backed up by a step-by-step project with plants that have been specifically chosen because they thrive in shaded spots.

? *Do you have a shaded, water-retentive area of garden?*

The solution is to plant species such as ferns, which thrive in this type of environment. *Right:* This royal fern enjoys the damp, acid conditions in the shade of the trees. SEE *Bed for a Moist, Shaded Site, page 140.*

➤ ∙ ➤ ∙ ➤ ∙ ➤ ∙ ➤ ∙ ➤ ∙ ➤ ∙ ➤ ∙ ➤ ∙ ➤

❓ *Is a boundary wall or other vertical surface casting too much shade?*

Although high perimeter boundaries give you privacy, they also create shade and deprive plants of light. Reflect light into the area by painting the wall or fence a light color or by introducing mirrors. *Right:* Ferns, climbers, and a holly are reflected in the strategically placed mirror, maximizing the amount of light that reaches the area.

SEE *Adding Light to a Shaded Corner, page 142.*

❓ *Do you have a mature tree under which nothing grows well?*

Lack of light is not the only problem: the tree roots may also be taking all the available moisture out of the surrounding soil. You can minimize the problem by planting shade-tolerant species such as small woodland plants.

SEE *Planting Under a Tree, page 138.*

Planting Under a Tree
GROUND COVER FOR DRY SHADE

A TREE, ESPECIALLY a mature one, is possibly the greatest asset a garden can have. Like a living sculpture, it can give your garden a dramatic visual focus. It also brings a feeling of maturity and provides a haven for birds and other wildlife.

Trees are not without their problems, however. Plants growing in their shade can become straggly, and lawns develop bare patches. Trees also extract a lot of water and nutrients from the soil, so neighboring plants may suffer. Enrich the soil with compost or farmyard manure, add a slow-acting fertilizer, such as bone meal, and mulch to a depth of 3–4 in (7.5–10 cm) to help retain moisture. If your tree casts very dense shade, you may need to remove lower branches and thin out the canopy. If a branch is safely accessible, you can remove it yourself with a bow saw; otherwise hire an arborist. Large branches are best removed in late winter or spring, although cherry trees should be pruned in the summer.

Ground-cover plants that thrive in dry shade, such as alyssum or periwinkle, are an excellent solution to the problems caused by trees. They cover bare patches of lawn and provide an attractive carpet of flowers that brings added interest to the area.

Purple shades

Purple is a good choice for shaded situations, since it merges beautifully with shadows. Add a sprinkling of white flowers and variegated leaves to reflect some light. Plant busy Lizzies after the danger of frost has passed. In fall, add a handful or two of purple, spring-flowering crocus bulbs to fill any gaps.

1 *Heuchera micrantha* 'Palace Purple'

MAINTENANCE

• *Keep the area free of weeds. Once the plants have grown together to form a dense carpet, weeding will be reduced.*

• *Water the bed in hot, dry weather to compensate for the water removed by the tree's roots.*

• *Remove untidy or dead growth and mulch in fall or spring.*

3 Busy Lizzies (*Impatiens*) – white variety

2 Periwinkle (*Vinca minor*)

PROJECT PLANNER

TIME SCALE **1+ HOURS**

Tools and Materials

Pruning shears • Bow saw • Fork • Spade • Rake • Bone meal • Manure • Bark-chip or gravel mulch

1 *If necessary, remove any small and spindly branches growing from the main trunk using a sharp pair of pruning shears. Take care not to damage the bark on the tree trunk.*

2 *Remove the bulk of any large branches using a bow saw. Cut the branch from underneath, 3–6 in (7.5–15 cm) from the point where it joins the tree trunk.*

3 *Next, saw from above, 3 in (7.5 cm) further from the trunk. As you saw, the branch will split to the first cut without tearing the uncut branch.*

4 *Neaten the pruned branch, making a clean cut at its base. This is much easier with the main weight of the branch gone.*

5 *There may be a slightly swollen area left near the base of the branch. Leave this on the tree. Do not apply wound paint, since this may encourage disease.*

6 *Gently loosen the soil underneath the tree with a fork, taking care not to damage the roots.*

7 *Enrich the soil by forking in manure and bone meal.*

8 *Buy the plants. If you cannot plant them immediately, store them in a cool place and keep well watered.*

9 *Plant the plants (see page 32) and water thoroughly. Mulch with bark chips or gravel.*

Bed for a Moist, Shaded Site
WOODLAND FERNERY

IF YOU HAVE A MOIST, shaded corner in your garden, make the most of it by growing plants that thrive in these conditions. Woodland ferns are ideal – and, because many are dramatic-looking, they are visually strong enough to contrast with any areas of hard surfaces, such as rocks, paving, and walls.

Ferns more than make up for their lack of flowers by the attractiveness of their leaves, or fronds. Each spring fresh new fronds slowly unfurl and grow into beautiful arching stems of the finest filigree, like the lady fern (*Athyrium filix-femina*). The fronds of others, such as the hart's tongue fern (*Asplenium scolopendrium*), are undivided, handsome, and glossy. Many ferns are rampant and so make excellent ground-cover plants for semi-wild areas beneath trees or between shrubs. In fall, many ferns turn a soft rust color. Others, such as the soft shield fern (*Polystichum setiferum*), stay green through winter.

Most ferns need a rich, moist soil, although some will tolerate dry conditions and will even grow in shaded crevices in walls. There are a few species that require lime-free soil, but in general ferns are easygoing plants that suffer from few pests or diseases and need little care and attention.

Rocky fernery for acid, neutral, or alkaline soil

These ferns, suitable for most ordinary soil types, nestle between large rocks around a shaded paved area. Clumps of small, early spring bulbs growing among the unfurling fern fronds would increase interest early in the season.

1 *Adiantum pedatum*

2 Male fern
(*Dryopteris filix-mas*)

3 Shuttlecock fern
(*Matteuccia struthiopteris*)

PLANTING ALTERNATIVES

Fernery for lime-free soils

If your garden soil is acidic, then you have the opportunity to grow some of the lime-hating ferns, such as the magnificent royal fern (*Osmunda regalis*). To show such a large fern off to its best advantage, reduce the scale of the neighboring plants. *Cryptogramma crispa* and the hardy maidenhair fern are both relatively small plants. Substitute the ferns listed here for those shown in the illustration below.

2 *Cryptogramma crispa*

3 Royal fern (*Osmunda regalis*)

4 Hardy maidenhair fern (*Adiantum venustum*)

PROJECT PLANNER

TIME SCALE **1 DAY**

Tools and Materials

Fork • Rake • Manure • Large rocks to match the color of surrounding paving • Trowel• Well-rotted compost • Bone meal • Bark-chip mulch
The time scale above is for a site about 6 x 6 ft (2 x 2 m).

1 *Mark out the shape of the new bed and prepare the soil (see page 46).*

2 *Buy some large rocks or collect them from around the garden. Set them into the soil so that they look natural.*

3 *Buy the plants. Stand them in the shade and keep the soil moist until you plant them.*

4 *Set the plants in position. Plant the large shuttlecock fern first, as this is the most prominent fern in the planting, and then the medium-sized male and soft shield ferns. Then put in the hart's tongue ferns and the adiantums. Plant the little blechnum ferns wherever there are gaps.*

5 *Before refilling the planting holes with soil, fork compost and bone meal in and around the planting holes.*

6 *Water thoroughly and scatter a bark-chip mulch around the base of each fern and over any bare soil.*

6 Hart's tongue fern
(*Asplenium scolopendrium*)

4 Soft shield fern
(*Polystichum setiferum*)

5 *Blechnum penna-marina*

MAINTENANCE

• *Water ferns in warm, dry weather. The soil should be kept moist but not waterlogged.*

• *Cut back dead fronds in fall using pruning shears. Evergreen fern species should be cut back in spring to make way for new growth.*

• *Weed regularly.*

• *Remove the young fronds of any ferns that are growing in the wrong place to keep your planting neat.*

• *Replenish the bark-chip mulch in late spring after sprinkling a little bone meal around the base of each plant or in fall before the first frosts set in.*

Adding Light to a Shaded Corner
MIRROR MIRAGE

MIRRORS ARE AN easy way of reflecting light into a shaded area of the garden. They have the additional benefit of making your garden seem larger and doubling the number of plants growing near by, giving the impression of lush and luxuriant growth. The illusion is even more effective when surrounding walls or fences are painted a light color. However, even though a mirror will bring more light to your plants, you still need to choose shade-tolerant species, since the extra light may not dramatically alter the overall growing conditions.

In front of the mirror, grow plants that have small, feathery, or divided leaves so that you can catch glimpses of the glass and reflections through them. Avoid dense, bushy plants that would produce a solid screen. Train climbers or wall shrubs along the mirror to overlap and disguise its straight edges.

Before you put up a mirror, experiment to find the best place for it. Observe the area throughout the day to discover when and where the light falls. See what view is reflected back, and decide whether the reflection could be made more interesting by positioning a plant, a pot, or even a garden statue in front of the mirror.

Light, bright planting for dry, neutral-to-alkaline soil

White paint and mirrors were used here to cheer up a dark house wall. In this planting scheme, tall Japanese anemones (Anemone x hybrida) *and dramatic spires of bear's breeches are reflected in the glass.*

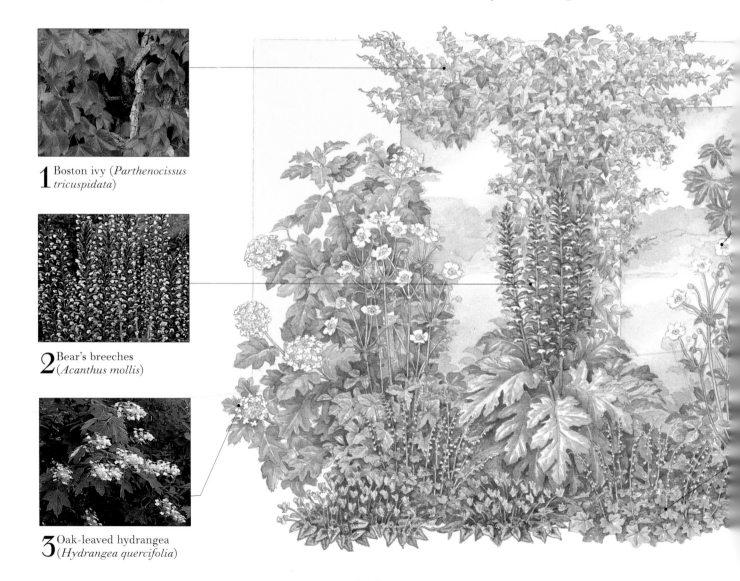

1 Boston ivy (*Parthenocissus tricuspidata*)

2 Bear's breeches (*Acanthus mollis*)

3 Oak-leaved hydrangea (*Hydrangea quercifolia*)

MAINTENANCE

• *Wipe the mirror once a month with a damp cloth.*

• *Remove any leaves or branches that obscure the mirror.*

• *Cut the stems of anemones and bear's breeches back to ground level once flowers are past their best.*

• *The reflective silvering behind the glass will gradually wear away and you may need to replace the mirror.*

4 Japanese anemone
(*Anemone* x *hybrida*)

5 Japanese aralia
(*Fatsia japonica*)

6 Fringecup
(*Tellima grandiflora*)

7 Ivy-leafed cyclamen
(*Cyclamen hederifolium*)

PROJECT PLANNER

TIME SCALE 1+ HOURS

Tools and Materials

Pencil • Spirit level • Mirror, predrilled in corners • Drill and appropriate drill bit • Anchors • Rubber washers • Screws • Screwdriver

1 *Clean up the wall or fence on which you are going to position the mirror. Fill any holes, if necessary, and paint the wall a light color, if desired.*

2 *Using a spirit level and a pencil, mark the positions of the screw holes on the wall or fence so that they correspond to the holes in the corners of the mirror.*

3 *Using the appropriate drill bit, drill holes in the wall or fence, and insert one anchor into each one. Inset: Position a rubber washer over the first hole and hold it in place.*

4 *Insert each screw through a rubber washer and into the one you fixed in the wall or fence behind. This washer holds the mirror away from the wall and prevents it from cracking.*

5 *Prepare the bed (see page 46) and plant.*

6 *Water thoroughly.*

THEMED GARDENS

Sea of tranquility
In this tranquil, Japanese-style garden, pots of lush ferns, hostas, and a purple-leaved Japanese maple frame the shore, while water lilies and reeds decorate the pond.

HERB GARDENS

ERBS HAVE BEEN grown for centuries for their culinary, aromatic, cosmetic, and healing properties. Although some are grown for their foliage alone, there are many others that have wonderfully aromatic flowers and leaves, making them a delight to have in the garden.

You can, of course, intersperse herbs with other plants in your beds and borders, but creating a garden specifically for herbs – even if it's on a very small scale – means that the plants are all in one place when you need to use them. It is also aesthetically pleasing: many of the herbs that grow well together look good together, too, as they come from similar habitats in the wild.

The herb gardens in this section feature some of the most popular herbs for culinary and household uses. They also cover a range of situations, from herbs that you can grow indoors on your kitchen windowsill to a raised bed for herbs that like well-drained soil, so you can be sure of finding something that suits your particular requirements.

Herbal haven
Left: This garden is functional as well as visually appealing. Mounds of purple sage and frothy lady's mantle frame the path, leading to a magnificent clump of purple lupins.

147

Cook's Herb Bed

HERBS FOR YEAR-ROUND COOKING

HAVING A GOOD selection of fresh culinary herbs on hand can transform your cooking – but it is not just their taste that makes growing herbs a good idea: many of the plants are a joy to have in your garden. Rosemary, for example, is a delightful, bluish, gray-leaved plant that can be grown anywhere as a shrub. Thyme makes a useful edging plant, and you can choose whether to clip it into a hedge or leave it to make a softer shape. The feathery texture of dill makes it a beautiful foil to grow in front of brighter plants.

Other useful herbs include mint and basil but both should be grown separately (see pages 150 and 154).

If possible, make sure that your herbs are within easy reach of the kitchen and are growing close together; then, when you need a sprig or two of something to put in the soup, you'll be able to find it easily without having to fight your way through the flower beds. The bed shown below will provide a good range of basic herbs for everyday cooking, but if your family has a favorite herb be sure to make room for it.

Year-round herb garden

Here, in a sunny position, are the basic necessities for a good bouquet garni (bay, rosemary, thyme, and parsley). Other popular herbs – tarragon, sage, dill, and chives – complete this versatile herb bed. Pot marigold is not an important herb in cooking, but its bright orange flowers will help brighten up the bed. The whole group is held together visually by a low-growing hedge of clipped thyme.

4 Dill (*Anethum graveolens*)

5 Rosemary (*Rosmarinus officinalis*)

3 Bay (*Laurus nobilis*)

2 Chives (*Allium schoenoprasum*)

1 Thyme (*Thymus vulgaris*)

PLANTING ALTERNATIVES

Herbs for summer salads

For tasty and unusual summer salads, replace the bay cones with a mound of trimmed dwarf nasturtium. Grow a patch of rocket plants from seed in place of the rosemary, and plant two or three sorrel plants in place of the sage. The tarragon, pot marigold, parsley, chives, dill, and thyme remain since all have an important place in summer salads. Use the flowers of the marigold, both the leaves and the flowers of the nasturtium, and the leaves of everything else. Harvest a few leaves from each plant, chop and serve with lettuce.

3 Dwarf nasturtium (*Tropaeolum majus* 'Peach Melba')
5 Rocket (*Eruca vesicaria*)
8 Sorrel (*Rumex acetosa*)

6 Tarragon (*Artemisia dracunculus*)

7 Pot marigold (*Calendula officinalis*)

PROJECT PLANNER

TIME SCALE 1 DAY

Tools and Materials

Fork • Rake • Coarse sand (for poorly drained soils only) • Bone meal • Manure or garden compost • Trowel • Watering can or hose • Bark-chip mulch

1 *Measure and mark the site and prepare the bed for planting (see page 46). If your soil is heavy, add some coarse sand to improve drainage – many herbs dislike wet soil.*

2 *Buy the plants. If you can't plant them immediately, stand them in the shade and keep them watered.*

3 *Plant the clipped bays and the central rosemary first, and then the other herbs, incorporating bone meal and manure or garden compost into the planting holes. Insert the pot marigolds wherever there are any spaces. Edge the bed with thyme.*

4 *Water thoroughly after planting and mulch with bark chippings.*

MAINTENANCE

• *Keep the bed watered and weeded.*

• *Try to stop herbs from flowering since it wastes energy and may adversely affect the plant or the flavor. Snip off the flowering stems of chives at ground level as they are tough and inedible. With woody herbs, such as bay, thyme, rosemary, and sage, flowering matters less – although if you want to preserve herbs, it is always best to harvest the leaves before flowering. Allow the pot marigold to flower, but remove the dead heads as they fade.*

• *Prune the thyme hedge in late spring and summer to keep it tidy and to encourage dense growth.*

8 Sage (*Salvia officinalis*)

9 Parsley (*Petroselinum crispum*)

Bed for Invasive Herbs

MINT BED

MINTS GROW so vigorously that they quickly swamp any other plants in the same bed. This is the last thing you want in a well-ordered herb garden, but mints are such useful plants that it would be a shame to banish them from your garden altogether.

Fortunately, however, there are a number of ways to contain them. You can sink a bottomless bucket into the ground and plant mint inside it so that its roots cannot extend sideways. If you have already planted mint and you want to stop it from spreading, push terra-cotta or slate tiles into the ground around the clump, overlapping them so there are no gaps between.

Alternatively, as in the design below, make a separate bed and grow different sorts of mint without the risk of them swamping other less vigorous plants. Mints thrive in ordinary garden soil and do not need bright sunshine.

Mint miscellany

This mint border is in a narrow, lightly shaded strip running alongside a paved path. The mints are contained within their own little empire – only the creeping Corsican mint spills over into the paving gaps. The planting is symmetrical, with the tallest mint (the spearmint) standing in the center of the bed to provide a focal point for the planting. A small, bushy ginger mint on either side provides a contrast in form. Peppermint and apple mint frame the ends of the bed.

1 Peppermint
(*Mentha* x *piperata*)

2 Corsican mint
(*Mentha requienii*)

3 Spearmint
(*Mentha spicata* 'Crispa')

150

5 Ginger mint (*Mentha* x *gracilis*), shown here in flower in summer

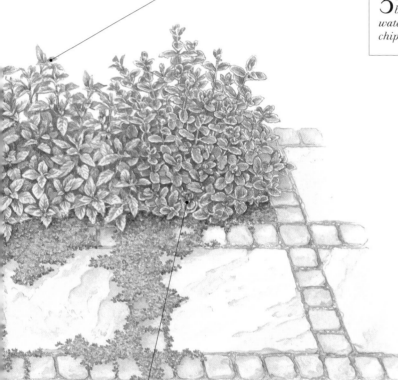

4 Apple mint (*Mentha suaveolens* 'Variegata')

PROJECT PLANNER

TIME SCALE **1 HOUR**

Tools and Materials

Fork • Spade • Rake • Bone meal • Manure • Trowel • Watering can or hose • Bark-chip mulch

1 *Buy the plants. If you cannot plant them immediately, stand them in the shade and keep them watered.*

2 *Prepare the bed for planting (see page 46), incorporating bone meal and manure into the soil. Plant the creeping Corsican mint plants in paving gaps or at the edge.*

3 *Set the remaining plants in position on the surface of the bed. When you are satisfied, plant them (see page 32), water thoroughly, and apply a 2-in (5-cm) layer of bark chippings over the bare gound as a mulch.*

MAINTENANCE

If one of the mints seems to be growing more strongly than the others, carefully lift it and plant it in a bucket that has holes in the bottom for drainage. The soil level should be 1 in (2.5 cm) below the rim of the bucket. Plant the bucket in the bed. This will prevent the mint from spreading and taking over the whole bed.

• *Harvest regularly. Use the leaves fresh or chop and freeze them with water in ice-cube trays to make mint-flavored ice cubes, which you can use to season stews or sauces.*

• *Cut back the mints to ground level in the fall.*

• *Lift, divide, and replant overcrowded plants in the fall.*

• *Keep the bed weeded and watered.*

Herbs for Well-drained Soil

RAISED HERB BED

WHETHER YOU WANT to grow herbs for household use, cooking, cosmetics, or medicinal purposes, you can create a beautiful herb feature from a raised bed. This will bring height to a large, flat area, such as an expanse of paving or lawn.

A raised bed is particularly suitable for herbs that dislike boggy conditions, since you can supply plenty of drainage beneath the soil. Treat a raised bed as you would any other container. Place a 3-in (7.5-cm) layer of drainage material, such as gravel or broken pots, at the bottom of the bed before covering with soil to make sure that water can drain away easily.

Old railroad supports are used in the illustration below. Alternatively, you could order new ones, cut to size, from good lumber stores. If you use wide, 10 in (25 cm) pieces of lumber to make the bed, you can sit on the edge and inhale the delicious scent of these aromatic plants.

Choose strongly scented herbs so that you can enjoy their fragrance as you walk past. The curry plant, lavender, thymes, and rosemary are all good examples.

Raised herb planter in purple, blue, and white

Rosemary, sage, and thyme billow over the edges of the bed, while the tall bright blue borage and white sweet rocket provide splashes of light and color. The borage and sweet rocket self-seed each year. The other herbs are perennials.

1 Rosemary
(Rosmarinus officinalis)

2 Borage
(Borago officinalis)

5 Sweet rocket (*Hesperis matronalis* 'Alba Plena')

4 Silver posie thyme (*Thymus vulgaris* 'Silver Posie')

PROJECT PLANNER

Tools and Materials

TIME SCALE 1/2 DAY

Old railroad supports or lumber 5 x 10 in (12.5 x 25 cm) cut to required length • Pointed, pressure-treated lumber pegs, 2 x 2 x 18 in (5 x 5 x 45 cm) • Mallet • 2-in (5-cm) galvanized nails • Hammer • Broken ceramic pots • Topsoil • Trowel • Watering can or hose • Gravel • Rake

1 *Plan the bed and calculate how much lumber you need. Order the correct lengths from a lumber yard.*

2 *Position the lumber, taking care to stagger the corner joints in order to make the structure stronger.*

3 *Drive wooden pegs into the ground inside the raised bed at each corner, flush with the timbers.*

4 *Nail the wooden pegs to the inside of the raised bed, using galvanized nails.*

5 *Place a 3-in (7.5-cm) layer of ceramic shards at the bottom of the bed and cover with top soil.*

6 *Plant the herbs (see page 32). Water thoroughly. Spread a thin covering of gravel around the bed and rake it level.*

3 Purple sage (*Salvia officinalis* 'Purpurascens')

MAINTENANCE

• *Keep the bed weeded and watered.*

• *In spring or summer, trim back any straggly stems of rosemary, sage, and thyme.*

• *Deadhead sweet rocket to encourage more flowers to grow. Allow one or two flowers to go to seed so that you will have plants next year.*

• *Remove the borage and the rocket in the fall.*

Potted Herbs
POT OF BASIL

ALTHOUGH MANY CULINARY herbs can easily be grown outdoors with a minimum of attention from the gardener, some of the most popular and useful ones need a little tender loving care. Basil is one such herb. It originates from the Indian subcontinent, where cold, wet summers are unheard of. In temperate regions, unless the temperature and soil conditions are exactly right, it can succumb to the cold and die. The solution to this problem is to grow it in a container, so that you can bring it inside if the weather suddenly turns cold.

Basil comes in many different varieties. There's the dramatic, dark purple-leaved basil, the small-leaved bush basil (the easiest to grow), the crinkly-leaved 'Green Ruffles', and Italian basil, renowned for its flavor. Grow a few to find out which you prefer. However, all basils like moist, well-drained soil, so remember to include plenty of drainage material in the container.

Three in one

The Italian basil in the center is the tallest of the three basils here, and gives some height to the display. It is also one of the mostly widely used basils in cooking. Around it are the lower-growing bush and purple-leaved basils. The purple basil provides a dramatic contrast in color to the other two.

1 Italian basil (*Ocimum basilicum* 'Genovese')

2 Bush basil (*Ocimum basilicum* var. *minimum*)

3 Purple-leaved basil (*Ocimum basilicum* 'Purpurascens')

154

PROJECT PLANNER

TIME SCALE 1 HOUR

Tools and Materials

Container • Gravel, pebbles, or ceramic shards • Potting soil • Water-retaining granules • Slow-release fertilizer granules • Watering can

1 *Place a layer of drainage material in the bottom of the container. You can use gravel, pebbles, or broken ceramic shards to promote drainage.*

2 *Fill the container with potting soil, incorporating water-retaining granules and slow-release fertilizer granules in accordance with the manufacturer's instructions.*

3 *Plant Italian basil in the center of the pot as it is the tallest. Plant purple-leaved basil at the front and back, and bush basil at either side to make the arrangement symmetrical.*

4 *Water thoroughly. If there is no danger of frost, the pot can be left outside. In cooler weather, keep it indoors in a sunny, draft-free spot.*

Pinch back the growing tips of the basil plants regularly to keep them bushy. You can use the pinchings in salads or sandwiches.

• *Keep the potting soil damp, but make sure water can drain away from the bottom of the pot.*

• *In cool weather, bring the pot indoors.*

Parsley pot

Parsley is another invaluable herb for the cook. It can be grown outdoors, but if you grow it in a pot you can bring it indoors in the fall and maintain your supply through the winter. Here, French marigolds are grown with the parsley as they are believed to deter pests such as whitefly. They also add a splash of color to the pot.

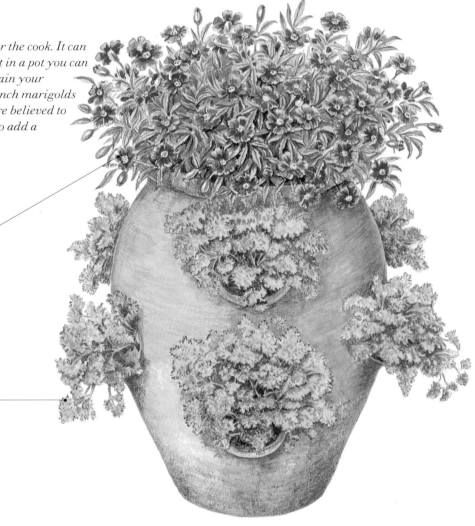

1 French marigold (*Tagetes patula* – bronze variety)

2 Parsley (*Petroselinum crispum*)

Herbs for Household Uses
HERB CORNER

ALTHOUGH WE TEND to think of herbs as something to use in cooking, they have many other uses: they can be used to make potpourri or soaps, delicious herbal teas, natural dyes, and natural pesticides or insect repellants. There are also a great many herbs that can be used for medicinal purposes — however, you should always seek your doctor's advice before using herbs medicinally.

The household herb bed shown below has plants that fall into all of these categories. One of the reasons why it looks so attractive is that all the plants, except the lavender, belong to the same plant family (the daisy family), and this gives the bed visual coherence. The lavender adds a contrast of color, form, and texture. Instructions on how to harvest and use the herbs are given in the chart opposite.

Household herbs with a silver, blue, and yellow theme

Here wormwood and cotton lavender (effective insect repellants) nestle between clumps of lavender (useful for making potpourri, soothing headaches, and keeping away houseflies and moths). The tall dyer's chamomile gives some height at the back of the bed and can be used as a yellow clothes dye. The flowers of the shorter chamomile make a great relaxing tea after a hard day's gardening.

4 Dyer's chamomile (*Anthemis tinctoria*)

3 Wormwood (*Artemisia* 'Powis Castle')

2 Chamomile (*Chamaemelum nobile*)

1 Cotton lavender (*Santolina chamaecyparissus* 'Lemon Queen')

Harvesting and Using Household Herbs

Chamomile
Use the flowers to make tea. Harvest the flowers when they open in summer. Put half a cup of flower heads into a teapot with four cups of water, cover with a cup of boiling water, and infuse for five minutes, then strain. Other herbs that can be used in this way include mint, fennel, and honeysuckle flowers.

Cotton lavender
Use to deter clothes moths. Pick sprigs of leaves and flowers in summer, tie in bunches and hang them up in a warm, dry place until they are brittle. Place a handful of dried leaves and flowers in a small muslin bag. Other herbs that can be used in this way include lavender, wormwood (see below), and alecost.

Dyer's chamomile
Use to dye natural fabrics. Harvest flowers in the summer. Chop them up and place them in a muslin bag. Put the bag in a bowl, pour over hot water, and leave to soak overnight. Transfer the bag and water to a pot and boil for about one hour. Remove and discard the bag. Boil the fabric you are dyeing in the liquid for an hour, stirring regularly. Allow to cool. Remove the fabric and rinse until the water runs clear. Do a final rinse in hot, salted water to help fix the color. Always wash fabric dyed in this way separately from the rest of your wash in cold water in case the color runs. Other herbs that can be used in this way include meadowsweet (black dye), sorrel (pink dye), and elder (purple dye).

Lavender
Use to deter houseflies, moths, and other insects. Harvest the flowers on long stalks as they open. Dry and use as for cotton lavender. Other herbs that can be used in this way include wormwood (see below) and alecost.

Wormwood
Use to repel clothes moths and other insects. Pick flowers and leaves in summer. Dry and use as for cotton lavender. Other herbs that can be used in the same way include lavender (see above) and alecost.

PROJECT PLANNER

TIME SCALE
1+
HOURS

Tools and Materials
Fork • Rake • Compost or manure • Trowel • Watering can or hose • Bark-chip mulch

1 *Buy the plants. If you are not able to plant immediately, stand them in a shaded place and keep them watered.*

2 *Prepare the bed (see page 46) and plant the plants, starting at the back of the bed and working forward.*

3 *Water thoroughly, then mulch with bark chippings.*

PLANTING ALTERNATIVES

Household herbs with a gold theme
Replace the cotton lavender with feverfew – an infusion of this has antibacterial properties and can be used to wipe down surfaces in the kitchen or bathroom. Change the chamomile for yarrow, which is a great compost activator and speeds up decomposition dramatically. Instead of dyer's chamomile, plant pyrethrum – the powdered, dried flowerheads can be used as an insecticide and are effective against aphids, ants, bed bugs, cockroaches, flies, mosquitoes, and spider mites. Replace the lavender with tansy, which deters ants and mice; place a few sprigs of dried tansy under your carpets. Wormwood remains to fill out the center of the bed.

1 Feverfew (*Tanacetum parthenium* 'Aureum')

2 Yarrow (*Achillea* 'Coronation Gold')

4 Pyrethrum (*Tanacetum coccineum*)

5 Tansy (*Tanacetum vulgare*)

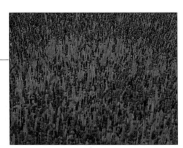

5 Lavender (*Lavandula angustifolia* 'Hidcote')

MAINTENANCE

• *Keep the plants watered and weeded.*

• *Tidy the bed in fall and apply a layer of compost or farmyard manure.*

WILDFLOWER GARDENS

YOU CAN MAKE A super contribution to the environment by dedicating even a small part of your garden to local wild flowers. As well as preserving flowers that might be under threat, you will also be encouraging wildlife into your garden in search of food and shelter. An added bonus for the weekend gardener is that wildflower gardens generally require less routine maintenance than more formal planting schemes.

Never dig up flowers from the wild; instead, make a note of what thrives in your local hedgerows and fields and buy seed or plants from your local garden center or a mail-order catalog. The wildflower gardens in this section feature plants that are suitable for a number of different habitats, from a hot, dry, prairielike site to a temperate wildflower meadow.

Flowering wilderness
Left: Here, a mixture of hedge parsley, scarlet poppies, and blue-stemmed grasses creates an inviting habitat for butterflies, bees, and other wildlife.

Wildflower Meadow
SPRING-FLOWERING LAWN

THERE CAN BE FEW more evocative sights than a grassy field dotted with colorful native flowers. Converting part, if not all, of your lawn into a meadow may help to restore the population of some rare plants in your area and encourage birds and other wildlife to visit your garden.

Grow young wildflower plants in bare patches (or seed bare patches) and stop mowing to allow them to colonize. If your lawn is in good condition, you will need to weaken the grasses to allow room for meadow plants to develop. Stop using fertilizers and weedkillers a season before you plan to plant, and mow as normal.

A spring-flowering meadow, such as the one below, should be mown for the first time in midsummer, after the flowers have set seed. For a summer-flowering meadow, with species such as ox-eye daisies and harebells, keep the grass down to about 3 in (7.5 cm) until late spring and then allow it to grow so that the wild flowers will develop. Scythe down the grasses and flowers in the fall and rake up the dried debris.

Meadow magic

A mown path leads to a rustic bench that is surrounded by flowers from early spring until early summer. Drifts of delicate blue, white, and pink flowers border the path, with elegant, bright yellow meadow buttercups providing a splash of brighter color behind the bench. In the background, the leaves of the wild daffodil, which flowers earlier in the year, are dying back.

1 Wild daffodil (*Narcissus pseudonarcissus*)

2 Meadow buttercup (*Ranunculus acris*)

3 Lady's smock (*Cardamine pratensis*)

4 Bladder campion (*Silene vulgaris*)

5 Germander speedwell
(*Veronica chamaedrys*)

PROJECT PLANNER

TIME SCALE 1/2 DAY

Tools and Materials

Trowel or bulb planter • Hand fork • Watering can with a fine rose spout attachment

1 *At least one season before you plant your meadow, stop using fertilizers and weedkillers of any sort. If your lawn is in good condition, continue mowing, but remove grass clippings since these return grass nutrients to the soil.*

2 *Buy some meadow plants or raise some from seed in pots. Choose local species: visit local wild areas to identify likely candidates for your own garden but never dig up or take seed from plants in the wild.*

3 *Use a trowel or bulb planter to remove a core of turf (see page 31). Place each plant in position, firm it in, and water.*

4 *Using a hand fork, loosen the soil surface of any bare patches and sprinkle on wild-flower seeds. In dry weather, water with a watering can with a fine rose spout attachment.*

MAINTENANCE

Cut the grass in mid- or late summer using a sickle or a weed whacker, then resume regular mowing until the grass stops growing in the late fall.

Allow the cuttings to dry in the sun before you rake them up.

• *If your lawn develops bare patches, sprinkle a few annual wildflower seeds, such as corncockle or poppies. Loosen the soil surface with a hand fork and sprinkle on the seed. Cover the seeds with chicken wire to prevent birds and animals from getting at them. Remove the chicken wire when the plants are established.*

Wild Flowers to Attract Insects

NECTAR-RICH TROUGH

MANY GARDENERS aim to encourage butterflies, bees, and other insects into the garden. Fascinating to watch in their own right, they also attract birds and small mammals.

Butterflies, bees, and many other flying insects tend to visit flowers that produce plenty of sweet nectar. The flowers do not have to be wild species; insects find many cultivated plants extremely attractive. Popular shrubs, such as the butterfly bush (*Buddleia davidii*), lavender, and marjoram, are all magnets for many species of butterfly.

If your space is limited, plant a container of nectar-rich plants. Position it in a sunny, sheltered spot (butterflies like still air, and a sunny area is always better for flowers than a shaded one). The ideal container is one large enough to create a mini-habitat, which also looks rough and natural – an old stone or concrete trough, for example. If you cannot get hold of an old container, paint a new concrete one with a watery solution of manure to encourage mosses and lichens to grow on it and speed up the aging process.

In the pink

This weathered concrete trough, with its nectar-rich, pink- and purple-flowered plants, will attract butterflies, bees, and other insects throughout the summer. The ice plant brings height to the group. Its gray foliage and pink flowers are repeated in the garden pinks in the foreground. Spilling over the front of the trough in front of the cushion of pink-flowered cranesbill is the purple-flowered creeping thyme.

1 Ice plant (*Sedum spectabile* 'Brilliant')

2 Pink (*Dianthus plumarius*)

PLANTING ALTERNATIVES

Yellow and orange theme

Insects are drawn to flowers by their colors as well as by their scent. Change the predominant color of your planting and you are likely to attract a slightly different range of insects. This orange and yellow scheme will attract hoverflies – their larvae eat greenfly, making them a useful pest control. In place of the ice plant, use yellow-flowered evening primrose. Change the pinks to orange French marigolds, substitute yellow alyssum for the thyme and yellow-flowered gold-moss sedum for the cranesbill.

1 Evening primrose (*Oenothera perennis*)
2 French marigold (*Tagetes patula*)
3 Yellow alyssum (*Aurinaria saxatile*)
4 Gold-moss sedum (*Sedum acre*)

4 Blood-red cranesbill
(*Geranium sanguineum* var. *striatum*)

PROJECT PLANNER

TIME SCALE 1/2 DAY

Tools and Materials

Container • Broken ceramic shards • Potting soil • Slow-release fertilizer granules • Water-retaining granules • Trowel • Watering can or hose • Gravel mulch

1 *Position the container in a sunny place, making sure that any excess water can drain away from the drainage hole under the pot. If necessary, stand the pot on small blocks of wood to allow water to drain away easily.*

2 *Buy the plants. If you cannot plant them in the container immediately, stand them in a shaded place and keep them watered.*

3 *Plant the container, putting a layer of ceramic shards in the base for drainage and incorporating fertilizer and water-retaining granules into the potting soil in accordance with the manufacturer's instructions (see page 30).*

4 *Water thoroughly and scatter a gravel mulch over the soil.*

MAINTENANCE

• *Keep the trough weeded and watered.*

• *Replenish the gravel as necessary.*

• *Snip off any dead or unwanted growth.*

• *Remove dead flowers once they've faded to encourage more to grow. Ice plant flowers can be left through the winter since they look attractive as they dry out.*

3 Creeping thyme (*Thymus praecox*)

163

Hot, Dry Wildflower Garden

PRAIRIE GARDEN

IF YOUR GARDEN is sunny, hot, and dry in summer and you want a natural-looking planting that requires relatively little maintenance, then a prairie garden is the ideal choice. This type of garden is dominated by grasses and vigorous perennials — hence the idea of the "prairie," where grasses dominate. They should be planted in widely spaced clumps, incorporating only half the amount of manure or fertilizer that you would normally use when creating a new bed, since a rich soil would encourage weeds. A sprinkling of gravel and a rocky path add to the prairie-like atmosphere. The planting shown below would look wonderful alongside a sun-baked gravel driveway.

Part of the fascination of this type of garden is the way in which it evolves over the years. Unlike most gardens, in which the gardener removes any weeds that compete for space, water, and nutrients, in a prairie garden the plants are left virtually to fend for themselves (see Maintenance, opposite). Within a few years, clumps of native grasses and wild flowers will grow up to cover most of the bare ground.

Drift of gold and purple

Here, clumps of strong-growing perennials and grasses, with gold and purple flowers, grow in a bed mulched with gravel. The gravel and the flat rocks set at intervals around the bed echo the natural prairie habitat that these plants would enjoy in the wild.

3 *Eryngium agavifolium*

2 Butterfly weed
(*Asclepias tuberosa*)

1 Gay feather
(*Liatris spicata*)

MAINTENANCE

• *In the first growing season after planting, keep the plants free of weeds. In subsequent years you can reduce the weeding. Once the plants are well established, you can leave them to fend for themselves, although you should always weed out any vigorous weeds, such as ground elder, dandelion, bindweed, or couch grass.*

• *In late fall, once the flowers are over and the bed is past its best, use a scythe to cut the growth down to ground level. Choose a dry day, so you can rake the debris away easily.*

4 Queen of the prairie
(*Filipendula rubra*)

5 Tufted hair grass
(*Deschampsia caespitosa* 'Golden Veil')

6 *Aster x frickartii* 'Mönch'

7 Switch grass
(*Panicum virgatum*)

PROJECT PLANNER

TIME SCALE 1 DAY

Tools and Materials

Fork • Rake • Spade • Rocks • Compost, garden manure or bone meal • Watering can or hose • Gravel or pebbles

1 *Buy the plants. If you can't plant them immediately, put them in a shaded spot and keep them watered.*

2 *Prepare the ground thoroughly (see page 46) and set rocks in position to create a natural-looking path through the "prairie."*

3 *Plant the plants, incorporating half the usual amount of bone meal, compost, or manure in the planting holes.*

4 *Water thoroughly. Lightly mulch the bed with a layer of gravel or pebbles to give the garden the appearance of a natural-looking, parched, prairie landscape.*

PLANTING ALTERNATIVES

Drift of white and gold

For a dusty, more subtle color scheme, substitute white and gold flowers for the purple ones. For white flowers, replace the queen of the prairie with heartleaf crambe, which has a huge cloud of tiny white blooms, and one of the clumps of gay feather with white coneflower. To strengthen the gold colors in the planting, change the other clump of gay feather to *Rudbeckia submentosa*, which has yellow flowers, and the aster to golden rod. The grasses – the golden tufted hair grass, the virgin grass, and the butterfly weed – can remain, since their colors and textures blend well with the white- and gold-flowered plants. The *Eryngium agavifolium* can remain too, as its blue-gray leaves harmonize with the white flowers.

1 White coneflower (*Echinacea purpurea* 'White Swan') and *Rudbeckia submentosa*

4 Heartleaf crambe (*Crambe cordifolia*)

6 Golden rod (*Solidago* 'Goldenmosa')

165

WOODLAND GARDENS

L EAFY TREES, SHRUBBY undergrowth, and a ground covering of bulbs and shade-loving perennials: these are the conditions normally associated with wooded areas. But even if you don't have mature trees, you can still have a woodland-style garden all of your own. Your garden may have conditions very similar to those in a woodland: it may be shaded by neighboring buildings, for example. The same plants thrive in both situations, so you can create the mood and feel of a woodland without the trees!

In this section, you will find a planting scheme for the center of a woodland area as well as one for the woodland edges. There are also instructions on how to create a natural-looking bark path, edged with spring-flowering bulbs.

Shady spot
*Left: This woodland is home to plants that revel in shade.
The rounded leaves of the pink-flowered bergenia, the
blue-green leaves of the hosta, and the fresh fern foliage
create an impressive display beneath the trees.*

Miniature Woodland

WILDLIFE HAVEN

IMAGINE A COOL, shaded woodland all of your own, where you can sit and escape from the heat of mid-summer. Contrary to what you might expect, you don't need acres of land or even existing mature trees. You can easily create a small-scale woodland from an existing shady shrub border. Just thin out the plants, add a tree or two, and plant some woodland ground cover. Choose small tree species if your space is limited. Silver birch, hawthorn, mountain ash, and crab apple are all suitable for small gardens and will attract a wide range of insects and bird life. For larger areas, plant a few oaks among the smaller trees for future generations to enjoy.

Encourage wildlife into your woodland by including features such as bird feeding tables, log piles to provide shelter for insects and small mammals, and nesting boxes for birds and bats. Always position nesting boxes in a shaded place, since they can overheat when the sun shines directly on them. Attach them firmly to a mature tree at least 5 ft (1.5 m) above the ground.

Woodland species for chalk soil

Chalk-tolerant species cover the ground beneath a spreading field maple and a spring-flowering Viburnum plicatum. *The hellebore provides long-lived flowers in early spring, followed by the sweet violets from early to mid-spring, and the variegated deadnettle in summer. In late summer and fall, the graceful white wands of bugbane sway gently in the breeze. The bird house will provide a safe haven from cats and other potential predators.*

1 Bugbane (*Cimifuga simplex*), shown here in flower in late summer

2 Stinking hellebore (*Helleborus foetidus*)

6 Field maple
(Acer campestre)

5 Sweet violet
(Viola odorata)

4 *Viburnum plicatum*
'Mariesii'

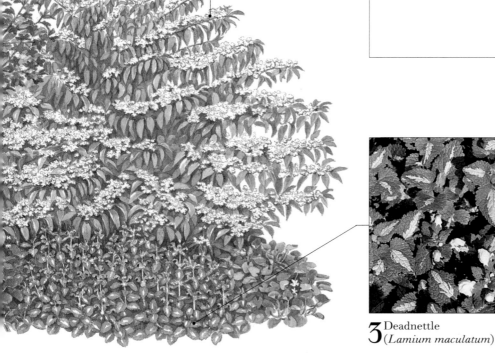

PROJECT PLANNER

TIME SCALE **1 DAY**

Tools and Materials

Spade • Fork • Rake • Compost or
farmyard manure • Tree stake and ties
• Trowel • Bark-chip mulch • Ruler
• Bird or bat nesting box • 2-in (5-cm)
galvanized nails • Hammer

1 *Prepare the area for planting as if you were making a new bed (see page 46).*

2 *Plant the field maple, using a stake to provide it with support in its early stages of growth (see page 33).*

3 *Plant the viburnum and other plants. Water thoroughly and mulch with bark chippings to help create an authentic woodland atmosphere.*

4 *Measure the width of the nesting box to check that it is not too wide for the tree.*

5 *Using a 2-in (5-cm) nail, nail the nesting box to the tree stake (if the tree is young) or to the trunk of the tree (if the tree is more than about 8 in/20 cm in circumference).*

MAINTENANCE

• *Keep the area weeded –
especially until the
ground-cover plants have
become established.*

• *Cut back any unwanted
growth to keep plants
within bounds.*

• *Replenish bark chip-
pings in late spring.*

• *Gently rake up any
leaves that fall from the
tree and shrub onto the
ground-cover plants.*

3 Deadnettle
(Lamium maculatum)

169

Woodland-edge Planting
DAPPLED SHADE GARDEN

THE PLANTS THAT do well on the edge of a woodland area are somewhat different than those that thrive in the center. A truly wooded area is heavily shaded for much of the year and thus requires plants that do well in shade. The woodland edge, on the other hand, has patchy sunlight, or dappled shade, most of the time and perhaps even full sun at some times of day. The soil tends to be fertile and damp, since — unlike the soil in a true woodland — it is not completely drained by tree roots or sheltered from rain by a dense overhead canopy of branches.

This means that you can choose from a much wider range of plants. For a natural-style planting use wild plants, such as the guelder rose, wild dog rose, foxgloves, ground-hugging primroses, ferns, and delicious wild strawberries. For a more cultivated look, shade-tolerant garden plants, such as hostas, candelabra primulas, and smoky-colored hellebores are all good choices. Alternatively, as in the illustration below, you can combine wild and garden flowers in the same planting. A mulch of bark helps to keep the weeds down and adds to the woodland atmosphere.

Leafy glade in purple and gold

In this colorful and lush planting scheme shown in early summer, towering purple foxgloves preside over yellow, orange, and purple candelabra primulas while cuckoo pint and Solomon's seal bring a quieter, more subdued feeling. Sweet violets seed themselves around the bed, cropping up here and there to provide a dense ground cover.

1 Solomon's seal
(*Polygonatum* x *hybridum*)

2 Sweet violet
(*Viola odorata*)

3 Cuckoo pint
(*Arum maculatum*)

4 Yellow candelabra primula
(*Primula prolifera*)

Foxglove
9 (*Digitalis purpurea*)

Shuttlecock fern
8 (*Matteuccia struthiopteris*)

PROJECT PLANNER

TIME SCALE **1/2 DAY**

Tools and Materials

Fork • Rake • Bone meal • Compost • Trowel • Bark-chip mulch

1 Prepare the area to be planted as if you were making a new bed (see page 46), enriching it with plenty of well-rotted compost.

2 Plant the largest plants first – the shuttlecock fern, lady's fern, Solomon's seal, foxgloves, and cuckoo pint. Then plant the primulas. Finally, fill in any gaps in the bed with the sweet violets.

3 Scatter a bark-chip mulch between the plants and around the bed.

Orange candelabra primula
7 (*Primula bulleyana*)

Lady's fern
6 (*Athyrium filix-femina*)

MAINTENANCE

• Keep the area weeded and water in dry warm weather.

• Watch out for slugs and snails – use traps and deterrents rather than slug pellets that may harm wildlife or pets (see page 36).

• Deadhead flowers as they fade.

• Cut back and remove dead growth in the fall before mulching.

Japanese candelabra
5 primula (*Primula japonica* 'Miller's Crimson')

Woodland Pathway

BARK PATH EDGED WITH BULBS

SUNNY SPRING mornings are the perfect time to enjoy a relaxing stroll along a winding woodland path. If you have a few trees, or even a few overgrown shrubs, you can create such a feature on a small scale in your own garden. All you have to do is lay a bark path that gently meanders its way through the undergrowth and winds along between the tree and shrub stems, and plant spring-flowering bulbs along the side of the path to define its edges. A prepared path is better than a dirt track, since it is less likely to turn to a slippery mass of mud in wet weather and weeds can be excluded more easily.

Many beautiful woodland bulbs, including the ones shown in the illustration below, flower in the spring so that they can take advantage of the period of spring warmth and sunlight before the tree canopy shades over the woodland floor. The bulbs will die back and disappear once they have flowered.

Drifts of white, blue, and yellow

Informal drifts of wake robins and purple-blue windflowers flop over the edge of a winding bark path, while behind them are waves of Spanish bluebells and sunny yellow erythroniums. Blue and white is a cool color combination that suits the shade of this tranquil woodland setting, while the small splash of yellow glows in the spring sunshine.

1 Spanish bluebell (*Hyacinthoides hispanica*)

2 Windflower (*Anemone blanda*)

4 *Erythronium* 'Pagoda'

MAINTENANCE

- *Weed and replenish the bark on the path as necessary.*

- *Allow the bulb foliage to die back naturally after flowering.*

- *After the bulbs have flowered, mulch the soil with compost or manure.*

3 Wake robin
(*Trillium grandiflorum*)

PROJECT PLANNER

TIME SCALE
1/2 DAY

Tools and Materials

Spade • Mallet • 4 pointed, pressure-treated lumber pegs, 2 x 2 x 18 in (5 x 5 x 45 cm) • Galvanized nails • 2 pressure-treated 5 x 1 x 36 in (12.5 x 2.5 x 100 cm) boards • Weed-barrier plastic • Wire pegs or skewers • Large bark chippings • Trowel or bulb planter
The timing given above is for a path about 10 yd (10 m) long

1 *Dig a trench for the path. It should be about 6 in (15 cm) deep and 1 yd (1 m) wide.*

2 *Using a mallet and peg, make four holes – one at each corner of the start and end of the path.*

3 *Make the path end units. Using galvanized nails, nail a peg to each end of the two boards.*

4 *Push the pegs into the holes made in step 2. Using a mallet, hammer the board and pegs level with the top of the trench. Lay weed-barrier plastic in the bottom of the trench. Push in wire pegs or skewers to hold it in place.*

5 *Fill the trench with bark chippings. Rake smooth.*

6 *Using a trowel or bulb planter, plant bulbs along each side of the path (see page 31).*

WATER GARDENS

A WATER GARDEN is one of the most peaceful and tranquil of all types of garden; the soothing sound of trickling water and the gentle buzz of insects make it a wonderful place for the weekend gardener to relax.

Once your water garden is in place, taking care of it is merely routine work. Although there is almost always some small task to do – fishing out excess pond weed, snipping off unwanted water lily leaves, tending any fish that you have in the pond – it is the sort of work that you can do out at your own pace.

The water gardens in this section give you a choice of formal and informal schemes and cover ponds, plants for a boggy area around a pond edge, and an easy-to-install decorative pebble fountain.

Peaceful pond
Left: This water garden, surrounded by woodland plants, will attract many passing birds and animals. A small-leaved water lily helps to keep the water clear, and the pink and purple flowers of the candelabra primula and foxgloves provide a burst of color to this tranquil scene.

Formal Pond
GARDEN GRANDEUR

A FORMAL GARDEN POND, topped by a dazzling white water lily, has a classic, stately elegance that evokes a mood of peace and tranquility.

Symmetry is the key to any formal design, so before you start digging make a plan of the site. If the pond is to be near the house, make sure that it is parallel to it and not set at an angle. Any surrounding paving should be symmetrical, too.

Ideally, the paving should overhang the pond so that the pond edge is not visible – but to do this, it is best if the slabs are cemented into position. A simpler method is to set the slabs on coarse sand and flush with the edge of the pond or overhanging the pond rim by no more than $^1/_2$ in (1.25 cm) – see opposite.

Pond garden in yellow and purple

The appeal of this pond lies in the contrasting shapes – spiky-leaved sweet flag and Japanese water iris, softly rounded kingcups and water lily. Around the edge are sun-loving caraway thyme, heartsease pansies, and New Zealand burr, all of which soften the paving.

7 Sweet flag (*Acorus calamus*)

6 Japanese water iris (*Iris ensata*)

1 Caraway thyme (*Thymus herba-barona*), shown here in flower in summer

2 Heartsease (*Viola tricolor*)

3 Kingcup (*Caltha palustris*)

4 White water lily (*Nymphaea* 'Virginalis')

MAINTENANCE

• *Keep the pond clear of blanket weed and other algae.*

• *Replenish the water in hot, dry weather.*

• *Remove the leaves of any water lilies that are over-crowded and pushing up out of the water.*

• *Remove dead leaves and other debris from the pond in the fall.*

• *If you have a pump, clean out the filter at least once a year.*

• *Remove any growth that is over-vigorous.*

5 New Zealand burr
(*Acaena microphylla*)

PROJECT PLANNER

TIME SCALE **2 DAYS**

Tools and Materials

Tape measure • Spirit level • Spade • Prefabricated fiber-glass pond • Coarse sand • Hose and water supply • Rake • Paving slabs • Car body putty • Gravel

1 *Dig the hole for the pond. The rim should sit at least 4 in (10 cm) below the hole's edge. Spread 2–3 in (5–7.5 cm) of coarse sand over the bottom.*

2 *Put the pond in the hole. Using a spirit level, check that it is level in every direction. Fill the pond with water.*

3 *Pack the sides with coarse sand. Push the sand down so that it goes under the pond shelf to support it.*

4 *Remove turf from the edge of the pond to fit the planned paved area. Inset: Spread a 2-in (5-cm) layer of coarse sand around the area to be paved and rake it level.*

5 *Arrange the paving slabs evenly around the pond to make an attractive design that involves no slab cutting.*

6 *Use a spirit level to check that each slab is level and in line with the preceding one. Add or take away sand as necessary to make the slab level and solid.*

7 *Spread car body putty on any visible liner on the edge of the pond and sprinkle gravel on top to hide the liner.*

8 *Plant any gaps in the paving with plants. Mulch with gravel. See page 31 for instructions on how to plant water plants.*

Plants for Moist Soil

BOG GARDEN

TALL ELEGANT FLAG irises in blue and yellow, the magnificent gunnera with its giant, umbrella-like leaves, stunning pure white arum lilies: these are just a few of the beautiful plants that you can grow if you have soil that is permanently moist.

In the wild, this situation occurs in a boggy area close to a slow-flowing river or stream. Few of us have a river or stream flowing through our garden, but you can recreate the same conditions by lining a bed with a perforated plastic sheet and covering it up with damp soil. Make it an irregular shape so that the boggy area looks like a natural, rather than a human-made, feature. Water the bed regularly to keep the soil permanently moist but not water-logged; a bark or pebble mulch will help to keep the soil moist. If you have a pond, it is even easier: make the surface of the bog garden slightly lower than the water level of the pond so that any overflow will dampen the bog.

Damp, leafy glade

This lightly shaded bog garden is dominated by the spiky leaves and large golden flowers of yellow flag and the smaller arching leaves of the orange-yellow daylily. At ground level, the heart-shaped golden-edged leaves of the two hostas soften the effect of the spiky-leaved plants.
A sea of purple bugle creeps around the edge of the bog and provides a dark, weed-excluding ground cover.

1 Purple variegated bugle (*Ajuga reptans* 'Atropurpurea')

2 *Hosta ventricosa* 'Aureomarginata'

3 Daylily (*Hemerocallis* 'Stella de Oro')

178

PROJECT PLANNER

TIME SCALE 2+ HOURS

Tools and Materials

Spade • Old carpet • Thick plastic sheet • Bricks • Fork • Soil • Compost or manure • Watering can or hose • Trowel • Bark-chip or pebble mulch

5 Yellow flag
(*Iris pseudacorus*)

1 *Dig out your bog garden, giving it a natural, flowing shape. It should be about 12–18 in (30–45 cm) deep in the center, shelving gently at the sides. Remove any exposed sharp stones.*

2 *Line the hole with a piece of old carpet, trimming it so that the edge extends over the edge of the hole by about 6 in (15 cm).*

3 *Spread the plastic sheet on top of the carpet and weight it down with bricks, trimming the edges to fit, if necessary. Pierce the plastic sheet with a garden fork so that excess water can drain away.*

4 *Fill the liner with good garden soil and fork in some compost or manure. Bring the soil level up to the surrounding ground. Make sure the liner is hidden from view.*

5 *Water the bog garden and leave it to settle for a day or two before planting.*

6 *Plant the plants and mulch with bark chippings or pebbles.*

4 *Hosta* 'Golden Tiara'

MAINTENANCE

• *Keep the soil moist, but not waterlogged. Check it regularly in hot weather.*

• *Keep the bog garden weeded. Don't let the bugle crowd out the other plants.*

• *Protect plants – particularly the hostas – from slugs and snails (see page 36).*

• *Deadhead the flowers once they are past their best to encourage more flowers to grow.*

• *Clean up and remove dead foliage in the fall.*

• *Apply a mulch of bark or pebbles in the fall.*

Water-garden Feature
PEBBLE FOUNTAIN

GURGLING WATER, glistening stones, lush green foliage: even the smallest garden has room for a decorative water feature such as this pebble fountain that comes as an easy-to-install kit.

Steer clear of true bog and water plants, as their roots need to be kept permanently moist. There are plenty of plants, such as hostas, some irises, and many ferns, that grow happily in normal soil but enjoy the cool, humid atmosphere created by the fountain.

For a natural look, spread pebbles or shells over the surrounding soil and between the plants. Many stones and shells have beautiful colors when wet; collect unusual ones when you're on vacation.

5 Soft shield fern
(*Polystichum setiferum* Divisilobum Group)

4 Lady's mantle
(*Alchemilla mollis*)

Shady sanctuary
Fern fronds and lady's mantle arch over the pebbles that surround the fountain and, with the Liriope muscari, *provide the taller elements of the planting. Foam flower and deadnettle spread over the gaps.*

1 Foam flower
(*Tiarella cordifolia*)

3 *Liriope muscari,* shown here in flower in late summer

PROJECT PLANNER

Tools and Materials

TIME SCALE **2+** HOURS

Spade • Old carpet • Pebble fountain kit (including submersible low-voltage pump, transformer, fountain, liner, and lid) • Spirit level • Bricks or stones • Pebbles or shells • Hose • Trowel • Gravel mulch

1 *Choose a level, sheltered site and clear the ground of plants and weeds.*

2 *Dig a hole slightly larger and deeper than the liner. Line the hole with a piece of old carpet to protect the plastic. Insert the liner and check that it is level.*

3 *Position the pump in the center of the liner and wedge it in position with bricks or stones. Follow the manufacturer's instructions to connect the pump to your power supply.*

4 *Put pebbles or shells in the base of the fountain. Fill the liner with water. Test the fountain and then turn it off.*

5 *Position pebbles or shells so that they hide the liner and the pump cable.*

6 *Plant up the surrounding area and mulch with a layer of gravel.*

PLANTING ALTERNATIVES

Sunny sizzlers

For a sunny spot, surround the pebble fountain with sun-loving plants. Replace the foam flower with a German iris, the liriope with red hot pokers, and the fern with a yellow-orange flowered daylily. Leave the lady's mantle, since it grows just as happily in sunshine. The white deadnettle is still useful, too, as a crevice-filler.

1 German iris (*Iris germanica*)

3 Red hot poker (*Knifophia* 'Samuel's Sensation')

5 Orange daylily (*Hemerocallis* 'Golden Chimes')

MAINTENANCE

• *Weed the plants surrounding the pebble fountain and water them in hot, dry weather.*

• *Remove any dead or dying flowers or foliage as it appears.*

• *Replenish the gravel mulch in fall or late spring.*

• *Maintain the fountain pump in accordance with the manufacturer's recommendations.*

2 White deadnettle (*Lamium maculatum* 'White Nancy')

Plants for Different Purposes

Here is a useful checklist of plants suitable for particular sites and for particular uses. The main season of interest is given for each plant; where no comment is made, the plant is grown for its attractive foliage. If a plant requires or prefers lime-free (acid) soil conditions, it is marked "A".

If several species and varieties within a particular genus are suitable for the purpose stated, then only the genus has been given. The genus *Hebe,* for example, includes several species and varieties that make suitable evergreen shrubs for containers – and so only the genus is noted in that particular list. Check the plant label or consult a plant encyclopedia to find out whether or not the species or variety you are planning to use is suitable.

If a particular species is listed (for example, the bay tree, *Laurus nobilis*), then this means that only this species – and, if it has them, most of its varieties or cultivars – is suitable. Sometimes a variety is not suitable for the purpose stated – it might be very vigorous or have an ungainly shape, for example – so always check before you buy.

Occasionally, a particular variety is specified on the list – for example, *Glechoma hederacea* 'Variegata'. This is either because it is the only plant commonly available or because it is the only variety of that species that is suitable for the purpose stated.

The lists that follow are based on the plants suggested for the projects in this book, with the addition of a small number of other useful plants.

Evergreen Shrubs for Containers

Potted evergreen shrubs can make an attractive feature for containers. They provide a leafy year-round backdrop to other plants; many are eyecatching enough to form a focal point in their own right.

Evergreen shrubs for containers in a sunny spot

Bay (*Laurus nobilis*)
Box (*Buxus sempervirens*)
Cotton lavender (*Santolina*) – summer flowers
Hebe – summer flowers
Jerusalem sage (*Phlomis fruticosa*) – summer flowers
Lavender (*Lavandula*) – summer flowers
Marjoram (*Origanum*) – summer flowers
New Zealand cabbage palm (*Cordyline australis*)
New Zealand flax (*Phormium tenax*)
Rose (*Rosa*) – summer flowers
Rosemary (*Rosmarinus officinalis*) – spring flowers
Sage (*Salvia officinalis*) – summer flowers

Yucca (*Yucca gloriosa*) – summer flowers
Thyme (*Thymus*) – summer flowers

Evergreen shrubs for containers in a shaded spot

Box (*Buxus sempervirens*)
Camellia (A) – winter or spring flowers
Cotoneaster – spring flowers; fall berries; some cotoneasters are evergreen
Euonymous (*E. fortunei*)
Japanese aralia (*Fatsia japonica*)
Rhododendron (A) – spring flowers

Perennials for Containers

Although perennials do not have as long a flowering season as bedding plants, there are a few hardy herbaceous perennials that look good and don't mind the cramped conditions of containers.

Perennials for containers in the shade

Bugle (*Ajuga*) – summer

flowers
Deadnettle (*Lamium*) – summer flowers
Elephant's ears (*Bergenia*) – spring flowers
Hellebore (*Helleborus*) – winter and early spring flowers
Heuchera – summer flowers
Hosta
Lady's mantle (*Alchemilla mollis*) – summer flowers
Soft shield fern (*Polystichum setiferum*)

Perennials for containers in the sun

Agapanthus
Catmint (*Nepeta*)
Hardy geranium (*Geranium*)
Iris
Pinks (*Dianthus*)
Sedge (*Carex*)

Herbs for Containers

It's often a good idea to grow herbs in containers positioned conveniently close to the kitchen so that you can reach them easily when you need them for cooking. Many herbs are shallow rooting and like

well-drained soil; growing them in containers is a relatively easy way of recreating their preferred growing conditions.

Herbs for containers in the sun

Bay (*Laurus nobilis*)
Chives (*Allium schoenoprasum*)
Lemon verbena (*Aloysia triphylla*)
Marjoram (*Origanum*)
Sage (*Salvia*)
Tarragon (*Artemisia*)
Thyme (*Thymus*)

Herbs for containers in shade

Basil (*Ocimum*)
Chervil (*Anthriscus cerefolium*)
Lovage (*Levisticum officinale*)
Mint (*Mentha*)
Parsley (*Petroselinum*)

Summer Bedding Plants for Containers

Each spring, many plants are offered by garden centers and

nurseries as temporary bedding plants. These are often specially bred varieties that have a long and prolific flowering season. Many are well suited to growing in containers. Most summer bedding plants grow best in a sunny place. However, there are a few bedding plants that tolerate shade.

Summer bedding plants for containers in the shade

Bedding lobelia (*L. erinus*)
Busy Lizzie (*Impatiens*)
Baby blue-eyes
    (*Nemophila*)
Flowering tobacco (*Nicotiana*)
Fuchsia
Monkey flower (*Mimulus*)
Nemesia
Pansy (*Viola* x *wittrockiana*)
Petunia

Summer bedding plants for containers in the sun

Bedding lobelia (*L. erinus*)
Cherry pie (*Heliotropium peruvianum*)
Diascia
Geranium (*Pelargonium*)
Ground ivy (*Glechoma hederacea* 'Variegata')
Helichrysum (*H. petiolare*)
Kingfisher daisy (*Felicia bergeriana*)
Marguerite daisy
    (*Argyranthemum frutescens*)
Marigold (*Tagetes*)
Morning glory (*Convolvulus*)
Nasturtium (*Tropaeolum majus*)
Snapdragon (*Antirrhinum*)
Wandering sailor
    (*Tradescantia fluminensis*)

Hardy Herbaceous Perennials

In general, hardy herbaceous perennials require a sunny

spot with fertile, moist but well-drained soil, and protection from strong winds. Given these conditions, there are many perennials that you can choose from. Tall to medium-height species should be planted towards the back of the bed and medium to low-growing ones towards the front. For shaded sites, shrubs and ground-cover plants are generally better.

Tall to medium-height perennials for sunny summer beds and borders

Aster (*Aster* x *frickartii*)
Bear's breeches (*Acanthus mollis*)
Butterfly weed (*Asclepias tuberosa*)
Daylily (*Hemerocallis*)
Euphorbia
Evening primrose (*Oenothera fruticosa*)
Gay feather (*Liatris spicata*)
Heartleaf crambe (*Crambe cordifolia*)
Japanese anemone
    (*Anemone* x *hybrida*)
Red hot poker (*Kniphofia*)
Sneezeweed (*Helenium*)
Switch grass (*Panicum virgatum*)
Tufted hair grass
    (*Deschampsia caespitosa*)

Medium-height to low-growing perennials for sunny summer borders

Catmint (*Nepeta* x *faassenii*) – evergreen
Deadnettle (*Lamium maculatum*) – summer flowers
Elephant's ears (*Bergenia*) – evergreen; spring flowers
Foamflower (*Tiarella cordifolia*) – summer flowers
Geranium – summer flowers
Heuchera (*H. micrantha*)

Ice plant (*Sedum spectabile*) – summer/fall flowers
Lady's mantle (*Alchemilla mollis*) – summer flowers
Lamb's ears (*Stachys byzantina*) – evergreen
Lirope (*L. muscari*) – fall flowers
Sweet rocket (*Hesperis matronalis*) – summer flowers
Yellow archangel (*Lamium galeobdolon*) – summer flowers

Weed-excluding Ground-cover Plants

Invaluable to the gardener with limited weeding or mowing time. Use in beds and borders to smother the ground between trees, shrubs, and perennials, or to cover an area that's awkward to mow. The plants listed below thrive in both sun and shade and tolerate a wide range of soil conditions.

Bistort (*Persicaria bistorta*) – evergreen; summer flowers
Bugle (*Ajuga reptans*) – summer flowers
Deadnettle (*Lamium maculatum*) – summer flowers
Elephant's ears (*Bergenia*) – evergreen; spring flowers
Foamflower (*Tiarella cordifolia*) – evergreen; summer flowers
Fringecups (*Tellima grandiflora*) – evergreen; summer flowers
Geranium – summer flowers
Heuchera – evergreen; summer flowers
Ivy (*Hedera helix*) – evergreen
Juniper (*J.* x *media*) – evergreen
Juniper (*J. squamata*) –

evergreen
Periwinkle (*Vinca minor*) – summer flowers

Self-seeding Annuals

Many plants cast their seed after they have flowered, and some of these will happily mature and flower without any help from the gardener. Among these self-seeding plants, the annuals are the most useful since they don't root deeply and deprive other plants of soil nutrients.

Alyssum (*Lobularia maritima*)
Borage (*Borago officinalis*)
California poppy (*Eschscholzia californica*)
Candytuft (*Iberis amara*)
Field poppy (*Papaver rhoeas*)
Heartsease (*Viola tricolor*)
Pot marigold (*Calendula officinalis*)
Snapdragon (*Antirrhinum majus*)
Welsh poppy (*Meconopsis cambrica*)

Easy-care Shrubs

Shrubs are the backbone of the low-maintenance garden. The shrubs listed below take very little looking after: virtually all you need to do is keep them tidy, weed free, well fed, and watered.

Easy-care shrubs for sun

Barberry (*Berberis*) – spring flowers; fall berries; some barberries are evergreen
Bay (*Laurus nobilis*) – evergreen
Cotoneaster – spring flowers; fall berries; some cotoneasters are evergreen
Cotton lavender (*Santolina*) – evergreen; summer flowers

Dogwood (*Cornus alba*) – winter stems

Hebe – evergreen

Jerusalem sage (*Phlomis fruticosa*) – evergreen; spring flowers

Juniper (*Juniperus*) – evergreen

Lavender (*Lavandula*) – evergreen; summer flowers

Mexican orange (*Choisya ternata*) – evergreen; spring flowers

New Zealand flax (*Phormium tenax*) – evergreen

Rosemary (*Rosmarinus officinalis*) – evergreen; spring flowers

Sage (*Salvia officinalis*) – evergreen; spring flowers

Smoke bush (*Cotinus coggygria*) – summer flowers

Yucca (*Y. filamentosa*) – evergreen; summer flowers

Viburnum – winter or spring flowers; some viburnums have berries in fall

Easy-care shrubs for shade

Camellia (A) – evergreen; winter or spring flowers

Cotoneaster – spring flowers; fall berries; some cotoneasters are evergreen

Japanese aralia (*Fatsia japonica*) – evergreen; fall flowers

Oak-leaved hydrangea (*Hydrangea quercifolia*) – summer flowers

Viburnum – winter or spring flowers; some viburnums have fall berries; some viburnums are evergreen

Hedging Plants

It's worth taking time to examine your soil conditions first, before you choose what to plant, to make sure you choose a species that will thrive in your garden. Some hedging plants can tolerate heavy soils; others require well-drained, lighter soils. The ultimate height of hedge that you require also affects your choice: consult a plant reference manual for this information before you buy. To edge a path or border, choose a hedging plant that is easy to keep under 2 ft (60 cm) in height.

Hedging plants that can tolerate heavy soils

Barberry (*Berberis*) – spring flowers; fall berries; some barberries are evergreen

Beech (*Fagus sylvatica*)

Cherry laurel (*Prunus laurocerasus*) – evergreen

Cotoneaster – spring flowers; fall berries; some cotoneasters are evergreen

Firethorn (*Pyracantha*) – evergreen; spring flowers; fall berries

Holly (*Ilex*) – evergreen; winter berries

Potentilla – summer flowers

Rugosa rose (*Rosa rugosa*)

Tassle bush (*Garrya elliptica*) – evergreen; spring catkins

Hedging plants that require well-drained soils

Camellia – evergreen; winter or spring flowers

Fuchsia – summer flowers

Hebe – evergreen; summer flowers

Shrub rose (*Rosa*) – summer flowers; fall fruits

Yew (*Taxus baccata*) – evergreen

Dwarf hedging plants

Box (*Buxus sempervirens*) – evergreen

Cotton lavender (*Santolina*) – evergreen; summer flowers

Hyssop (*Hyssopus vulgaris*) – evergreen

Lavender (*Lavandula*) – evergreen; summer flowers

Thyme (*Thymus vulgaris*) – evergreen

Climbing Plants

Some climbers flower well only in sun – although they may prefer to have their roots in shade. Others grow perfectly well in shaded conditions. Many climbing plants and wall shrubs – roses and clematis, for example – are best left to ramble freely over their support. Others can be clipped into shape and trained to make a more formal feature. For this sort of feature, choose climbing plants and wall shrubs that respond well to pruning; they have relatively small leaves that grow densely and so make a uniform pattern of growth.

Climbing plants that require sun (though roots may be shaded)

Actinidia kolomicta – leaves in summer

Clematis – flowers in spring, summer or fall; seedheads in fall; some clematis are evergreen

Crimson glory vine (*Vitis coignetiae*) – leaves in fall

Golden hop (*Humulus lupulus* 'Aureus') – flowers in fall

Honeysuckle (*Lonicera*) – flowers in spring or summer; some honeysuckles are evergreen

Morning glory (*Ipomoea rubrocaerulea*) – annual climber

Nasturtium (*Tropaeolum*) – annual climber

Rose (*Rosa*)

Sweet pea (*Lathryus odoratus*) – annual climber

Wisteria – summer flowers

Climbing plants that tolerate shade

Boston ivy (*Parthenocissus*) – leaves in fall

Climbing hydrangea (*Hydrangea anomala* ssp. *petiolaris*) – summer flowers

Firethorn (*Pyracantha*) – evergreen; spring flowers; fall berries

Honeysuckle (*Lonicera japonica* 'Halliana') – evergreen; flowers in spring

Ivy (*Hedera helix*) – evergreen

Oriental bittersweet (*Celastrus orbiculatus*)

Russian vine (*Fallopia baldschuanica*)

Virginia creeper (*Parthenocissus*) – leaves in fall

Climbing plants and wall shrubs suitable for training

California lilac (*Ceanothus*) – evergreen; spring, summer, or fall flowers

Euonymus – evergreen

Firethorn (*Pyracantha*) – evergreen; spring flowers; fall berries

Flowering quince (*Chaenomeles*) – spring flowers

Ivy (*Hedera helix*)

Scented Bedding Plants and Shrubs

Add another dimension to your garden by growing scented plants – particularly near sitting areas, or beside paths, where you will benefit from their fragrance every time you walk past.

Scented bedding plants

Flowering tobacco (*Nicotiana*)
Petunia — some varieties are scented
Stocks (*Matthiola*)
Sweet pea (*Lathyrus odoratus*) — some varieties are scented

Scented shrubs

Daphne — spring or summer flowers; some daphnes are evergreen
Lavender (*Lavandula*) — evergreen; summer flowers
Philadelphus — spring or summer flowers
Viburnum — winter or spring flowers, fall berries; some viburnums are evergreen
Witch hazel (*Hamamelis*) — winter or spring flowers

Bulbs Suitable for Naturalizing

Grow natural-looking drifts of spring, fall- or winter-flowering bulbs in your lawn or among trees and shrubs to mark the seasonal changes and add a splash of color to your garden when relatively few other plants are flowering. The bulbs listed below all multiply to form a growing colony.

Bluebell (*Hyacinthoides*) — spring flowers
Crocus — winter or spring flowers
Cyclamen — fall or winter flowers
Daffodil (*Narcissus*) — spring flowers
Erythronium — spring flowers
Fritillary (*Fritillaria*) — spring flowers

Glory-of-the-snow (*Chionodoxa*) — spring flowers
Lily-of-the-valley (*Convallaria*) — spring flowers
Scilla — spring flowers
Snowdrop (*Galanthus*) — winter or spring flowers
Wake robin (*Trillium*) — spring flowers
Windflower (*Anemone*) — spring flowers

Spring and Summer Meadow Flowers

The plants listed below thrive in a wide range of conditions, but with a little research you will soon discover your own local wildflower species.

Bladder campion (*Silene vulgaris*) — spring and summer flowers
Cornflower (*Centaurea cyanus*) — summer flowers
Daisy (*Bellis perennis*) — spring and summer flowers
Lady's smock (*Cardamine pratensis*) — spring flowers
Meadow buttercup (*Ranunculus acris*) — spring and summer flowers
Meadow cranesbill (*Geranium pratense*) — summer flowers
Ox-eye daisy (*Leucanthemum vulgare*) — summer flowers
Primrose (*Primula veris*) — spring flowers
Speedwell (*Veronica chamaedrys*) — spring and summer flowers
Yarrow (*Achillea millefolium*) — summer flowers

Trees for Small Gardens

A tree can transform your garden, but the wrong tree can damage your house as some species have wide-spreading root systems that can undermine buildings, wrap around and crack drains, or widen existing fractures in brickwork or concrete. Attractive trees that are not usually the cause of any damage belong to the plant groups listed below. Always check the ultimate height of a tree before you buy it and plant it the same distance away from any building; in that way, you can be reasonably sure that the roots will not damage your building.

Apple (*Malus*) — spring flowers; fall fruit
Mount Etna broom (*Genista aetnensis*) — summer flowers
Hazel (*Corylus avellana*) — spring flowers
Maple (*Acer*)
Mountain ash (*Sorbus*) — spring flowers; fall fruit
Pear (*Pyrus*) — spring flowers

Water Plants

Water plants vary in the depth of water that they prefer.

Pond plants that require more than 1 ft (30 cm) of water

Water hawthorn (*Aponogeton distachos*) — summer flowers
Water lily (*Nymphaea*) — summer flowers

Pond plants that thrive in 2–12 in (5–30 cm) of water

Cardinal flower (*Lobelia cardinalis*) — summer flowers
Dwarf cattail (*Typha minima*)
Golden club (*Orontium aquaticum*) — summer flowers
Japanese iris (*Iris laevigata*) — summer flowers
Kingcup (*Caltha palustris*) — summer flowers
Manna grass (*Glyceria maxima*)
Parrot's feather (*Myriophyllum aquaticum*)
Pygmy water lily (*Nymphaea pygmaea*) — summer flowers
Sweet flag (*Acorus calamus*) — summer flowers
Water lettuce (*Pistia stratiotes*)
Yellow flag (*Iris pseudacorus*) — summer flowers

Plants that grow in permanently moist soil

Bugle (*Ajuga*) — summer flowers
Cuckoo pint (*Arum maculatum*) — summer flowers
Daylily (*Hemerocallis*) — summer flowers
Hosta
Primula — summer flowers
Shuttlecock fern (*Matteuccia struthiopteris*)
Solomon's seal (*Polygonatum x hybridum*) — summer flowers

Index

Acknowledgments

I would like to thank all those people who have been involved in the production of this book – in particular, Ken Davis, without whom this book would not have been undertaken, for his help and general advice; Liz Dobbs for her contribution to the Gardening Basics section and the step-by-step photography; Phil Binks, Val Burton, Ruth Chivers, Anne de Verteuil, and Wendy Francis for their input on step-by-step photography; Brian Mathew and Janet Swarbrick for checking the plant photographs and nomenclature; Marie Lorimer for the index; to Hozelock Ltd for providing gardening equipment and to Stephen Morgan for supplying plants. Many thanks, too, to Sarah Hoggett, Julia Ward-Hastelow, Alison Lee and Corinne Asghar at Collins & Brown, for their diligence and patience.

Picture Credits

All the photographs in this book were specially taken by Sampson Lloyd, Geoff Dann and Mark Gatehouse for Collins & Brown, except the following:

page 1 Lynne Brotchie/The Garden Picture Library (GPL), page 2 Steven Wooster, page 5 Steven Wooster, page 6 bottom left, Steven Wooster, page 7 top left, top right, Steven Wooster, pages 12-13 Steven Wooster, page 35 John Glover/GPL, page 36 Brian Carter/GPL, Chris Burrows/GPL, Nigel Francis/GPL, JS Sira/GPL, page 37 Holt Studios International (Nigel Cattlin), Holt Studios International (Nigel Cattlin), Neil Holmes/GPL, Neil Holmes/GPL, Holt Studios International (Nigel Cattlin), pages 44-45 Holt Studios International, Brian Carter/GPL, pages 52-53 Steven Wooster pages 54-55 Steven Wooster, pages 56-57 1. Brian Carter/GPL 2. Patrick Mason/Collins & Brown 3. Andrew Lawson 4. Chris Burrows/GPL, pages 58-59 1. Clive Nichols/Old Rectory, Berkshire 2. John Glover/GPL 3. Patrick Mason 4. Chris Smith/Collins & Brown 5. A-Z Botanical Collection/Neil Joy 6. Harry Smith Collection, pages 60-61 1. J. S. Sira/GPL 2. Patrick Mason/Collins & Brown 3. Neil Holmes/GPL 4. Harry Smith Collection, pages 62-63 1. Andrew Lawson 2. Patrick Mason/Collins & Brown 3. Patrick Mason/Collins & Brown 4. Harry Smith Collection 5. Howard Rice/GPL pages 64-65 1. John Glover/GPL 2. Harry Smith Collection 3. Howard Rice 4. Patrick Mason/Collins & Brown, pages 66-67 1. Harry Smith Collection 2. Harry Smith Collection 3. Patrick Mason/Collins & Brown, 4. David Russell/GPL, pages 68-69 1. Patrick Mason 2. Brian Carter/GPL 3. Harry Smith Collection, pages 70-71 Ron Sutherland/GPL, page 72 Steven Wooster, page 73 Steven Wooster, Neil Campbell-Sharp, pages 78-79 1. Patrick Mason/Collins & Brown 2. Clive Nichols Garden Pictures 3. Clive Nichols Garden Pictures 4. Patrick Mason/Collins & Brown 5. Andrew Lawson, pages 84-85 Steven Wooster, pages 86-87 Steven Wooster, pages 88-89 1. Neil Holmes/GPL 2. Patrick Mason/Collins & Brown 3. Patrick Mason/Collins & Brown 4. Clive Nichols Garden Pictures, pages 90-91 1. Jacqui Hurst 2. Clive Nichols Garden Pictures 3. Andrew Lawson 4. Brian Carter/GPL, pages 92-93 1. Howard Rice 2. Patrick Mason/Collins & Brown 3. Vaughan Fleming/GPL, pages 98-99 Steven Wooster, pages 100-101 Steven Wooster, pages 102-103 1. Patrick Mason/Collins & Brown 2. Vaughan Fleming/GPL 3. Sampson Lloyd/Collins & Brown, pages 104-105 1. Clive Nichols Garden Pictures 2. Howard Rice/GPL 3. Patrick Mason/Collins & Brown, pages 106-107 1. Steven Wooster 2. Andrew Lawson 3. Neil Holmes/GPL 4. Patrick Mason/Collins & Brown, pages 108-109 1. Andrew Lawson 2. Patrick Mason 3. Patrick Mason/Collins & Brown, pages 110-111 1. Zara McCalmont/GPL 2. Andrew Lawson, pages 112-113 Patrick Mason/Collins & Brown, pages 114-115 Patrick Mason/Collins & Brown, pages 116-117 1. Andrew Lawson 2. Steven Wooster 3. Howard Rice, pages 118-119 Steven Wooster, pages 120-121 Steven Wooster, pages 122-123 Steven Wooster, pages 124-125 1. John Glover/GPL 2. Robert Estall/GPL 3. Harry Smith Collection 4. Andrew Lawson 5. Andrew Lawson 6. Patrick Mason/Collins & Brown 7. Chris Smith/Collins & Brown 8. Patrick Mason/Collins & Brown, pages 126-127 1.Harry Smith Collection, pages 128-129 1. Harry Smith Collection, 2. Brian Carter/GPL 3. A-Z Botanical Collection 4. Harry Smith Collection, pages 130-131 1. Harry Smith Collection 2. Chris Smith/Collins & Brown 3. David Askhan/GPL 4. Howard Rice/GPL 5. Jacqui Hurst, pages 132-133 1. Patrick Mason 2. Steven Wooster 3. Andrew Lawson 4. Howard Rice/GPL 5. Patrick Mason/Collins & Brown 6. Patrick Mason/Collins & Brown 7. Densey Clyne/GPL 8. Chris Smith/Collins & Brown 9. Patrick Mason/Collins & Brown, pages 134-135 1. Vaughan Fleming/GPL 2. Andrew Lawson 3. Clive Nichols/ GPL 4. Photos Horticultural 5. Patrick Mason/Collins & Brown 6. Howard Rice 7. Andrew Lawson 8. Chris Smith 9. Clive Nichols, pages 136-137 Steven Wooster, Neil Campbell-Sharp, pages 138-139 1. Patrick Mason/Collins & Brown 2. Christopher Fairweather/GPL 3. Chris Burrows/GPL, pages 140-141 1. John Glover/GPL 2. John Glover/GPL 3. Andrew Lawson 4. Steven Wooster 5. John Glover/GPL 6. Harry Smith Collection, pages 142-143 1. Clive Nichols/Dinmore Manor, Worcs 2. Andrew Lawson 3. Mayer/Le scanff/GPL 4. Chris Smith 5. Andrew Lawson 6. Andrew Lawson 7. Harry Smith Collection, pages 144-145 Steven Wooster, pages 146-147 Steven Wooster, pages 148-149 1. Jacqui Hurst 2. Harry Smith Collection 3. Andrew Lawson 4. Jerry Pavia/GPL 5. John Glover/GPL 6. Harry Smith Collection 7. Chris Smith/Collins & Brown 8. Jacqui Hurst/GPL 9. Juliette Wade/GPL, pages 150-151 1. John Glover/GPL 2. Vaughan Fleming/GPL 3. Patrick Mason/Collins & Brown 4. John Glover/GPL 5. Photos Horticultural, pages 152-153 1. John Glover/GPL 2. Juliette Wade/GPL 3. Patrick Mason/Collins & Brown 4. Andrew Lawson 5. Harry Smith Collection, page 154 1. Sampson Lloyd 2. Photos Horticultural 3. Joan Dear/GPL, page 155 1. Harry Smith Collection 2. Juliette Wade/GPL, pages 156-157 1. Harry Smith Collection 2. Harry Smith Collection 3. Patrick Mason/Collins & Brown 4. Patrick Mason/Collins & Brown 5. Steven Wooster, pages 158-159 Steven Wooster, pages 160-161 1. Didier Willery/GPL 2. Jacqui Hurst/GPL 3. Jacqui Hurst/GPL 4. Michael Howes/GPL 5. Geoff Dann/GPL, pages 162-163 1. Patrick Mason/Collins & Brown 2. Jerry Piava/GPL 3. Patrick Mason 4. Harry Smith Collection, pages 164-165 1. Patrick Mason/Collins & Brown, 2. Harry Smith Collection 3.Ron Sutherland/GPL 4. Clive Boursnell/GPL 5. Didier Willery/GPL 6. Chris Smith/Collins & Brown 7. Harry Smith Collection, pages 166-167 Steven Wooster, pages 168-169 1. Andrew Lawson 2. Clive Nichols Garden Pictures 3.Patrick Mason/Collins & Brown 4. Steven Wooster 5. Jacqui Hurst 6. Didier Willery/GPL, pages 170-171 1. Steven Wooster 2. Jacqui Hurst 3. Harry Smith Collection 4. Juliette Wade/GPL 5. Steven Wooster/GPL 6. Howard Rice/GPL 7. Howard Rice/GPL 8. Mayer/Le scanff/GPL 9. Steven Wooster, pages 172-173 1. Steven Wooster 2. Clive Nichols 3. Steven Wooster 4. Chris Smith, pages 174-175 Steven Wooster, pages 176-177 1. Jerry Pavia/GPL 2. Howard Rice 3. Andrew Lawson 4. A-Z Botanical Collection/Peter Etchells 5. Patrick Mason/Collins & Brown 6. Harry Smith Collection 7. Harry Smith Collection, pages 178-179 1. Steven Wooster/GPL 2 Patrick Mason 3. Patrick Mason/Collins & Brown 4. Steven Wooster 5. Jacqui Hurst, pages 180-181 1. Joan Dear/GPL 2. Patrick Mason/Collins & Brown 3. Clive Nichols Garden Pictures 4. Andrew Lawson 5. Steven Wooster

While every effort has been taken to ensure that all pictures have been fully and correctly credited, the publishers would be pleased to hear of any discrepancies or omissions.